AT THE DOOR
Visions In Excellence Journals

VIEWS

From Back Of The

PRAYER CLOSET

The 8-Day Devotional & Journey
To Greater Answers, Insights & Hope!

Ivory Stone

AT THE DOOR
Visions In Excellence Journals

DEDICATION & APPRECIATION

To God ~ my Lord and Father, my Friend and Teacher!
Thanks for Your eternal, life giving Words! Without them,
I would have nothing to say. By them, I know and believe
Your love for me. All my gratitude is born in You!

To my mother, Pastor Verletta Stone, who's heartbeat was
to help others, who so inspired my life by tirelessly impressing upon me the importance of faithing in God. I am forever
tempered by her determined, relentless love for all people,
and unwavering press for God.

To Kevin, my son, my blessing, and constant reminder that
God rewards for planting trust into faith! I am motivated by
your courage to leap over every obstacle.

To those who were examples of what to do, and not to do,
to the many lives God led me to follow and examine - men-
tors, teachers, encouragers and challengers, and by whom
I am enabled to be growing still.

To my fearless, bold prayer partner, Lydia Nicole, who has
never let me not believe God, or fail to have faith in myself.
Your contagious, miracle manifesting, 'Let's Pray!' mindset,
fuels my faith and God-fidence. I thank you for being a profound model of truth!

INTRODUCTION

Thanks for opening this book! It's full of empowerings from real, life-changing experiences. They are my very treasured wisdom keys to living by faith. Sharing them is my privileged duty, for by them I got to know God, to believe and trust Him, and grow to live my identity - the who God made me to be.

Within these pages are tells of the great power prayer is. Beyond its fuel to grow up my faith, the embryonic labors of my prayer efforts became a stability needed to seek Whom I now know as 'my' faithful Lord. Facing numbing challenges, with scary-enough-to-lose-my-mind events, I found in prayer such a power that was my lifeboat to living. It became the doorway to a peace I had no ability to comprehend. Simply, it was an invitation, from God, to talk to Him, and be heard by Him.

Life and its seasons brought me an array of circumstances allied to situations with faith defenders and doubt perpetrators. Yet God spun them into road markers to stay me on a path far from my own self-appointed horizons. These 'guides' were a gift, His Godsends, to dismantle mishaps imposing threats to my divine purpose. Many summoned by prayer, all given by grace, God's mercies and provisions morphed the hard places into profound conduits of change. His caregiving rescued me from the would-be shatterings of life itself.

We all meet people, churches, family, good, bad, dreaded unexpecteds. My encounters turned tools, chiseled away to reveal what I naively thought I needed. By prayer, I survived a melange of fears, bad returns on misplaced trusts, and other beat-you-in-your-cell wardens. What is marvelously sweet,

God <u>waits</u> to hear and answer the prayers of *anyone* who dares call Him for help or answers, by day or by the darkest night!

I thank God for His allowances of graces dispensed to me amid incredible wiles of known and unknown dangers. They kept me and my mind, speaking wisdom and hope to me. It is God Who heals, enabling the praying to stand, to walk sure-footed though fulsomely familiar with limping forward. It is this God Who humbled Himself to pick up every piece of my brokenness. He reset me, uprighting someone like me - a person told many times, by words and deeds, 'you're nobody', 'you are nothing'.

Often, I muffled my cries for help in back of my prayer closet to silence my fears. But, as God heard the blood of Abel whom Cain slew (Genesis 4:10), He heard me! He responded! When seeking answers I'd hoped to be my sought after resolves, my Omniscient Father drew me to receive <u>His answers</u>. I can attest finding them to always be the best resolves! He taught me what 'seems' right may be far from righteous, or just not good enough.

Those answers were His Father to child redirections. They were my relief and solace. They saved me from deceits, and veers off to nowhere. God redefined my prayer closet to be an 'any place' I am, and 'any time' I call to Him. He will answer whosoever calls, needs Him, or wants to bask In His presence.

This phenomenal journey of prayer led me to find myself in Him, a far place from a devalued victim of stolen worth. Isn't that just like a real, true, loving father? In all my priors, I had never known such a thing as a father's love. Father God does such a thing so very well, so crazy good, and always with tender love and grace.

Prayer is God's beautiful, lovingly clever way of talking 'with' us. By it He cares for us, walking into our rooms and difficulties, all our hurts and crazies. With this spiritual communique and holy gift comes relationship ~ <u>what He longs for</u>. By this connection grace to God, covenant partnership forges inviting God, with all of His power, into our whole life! With absolute love, He brings to speech the enablement of His response that we may experience Him! Therein is 'the call' to share the supernatural beauty of this free, liberating, unmerited prize that prayer is with others! For these reasons, and your sake, I pen this book!

I encourage you to get locked down and lost in God's love, and the constancy of His unfathomable faithfulness. To begin, say His Name ~ Jesus! By every measure, that <u>is</u> prayer! It is your summons for His holy presence - His intrusion into whatever or whoever dares oppose you. There you will learn strengths that release His Word of Power, the Holy Bible, to invade any place or challenge, and to heal your whole life. You'll find it stunning!

For sure, life can be hard. Its challenges and uncertain returns can bring us to lesser places and tears. That's why God has a plan for us to know Him and receive <u>His</u> real life. It ought to be an easy 'yes' considering all His other plans still work, like days following nights. Clearly, His ways of doing are extraordinarily credible. It would be wise to choose what God offers by way of His Abundant Life Plan - a promise of good success, purposed, created, and intentionally crafted especially for you!

My prayer is that your best days and your best life would begin in this now, in this moment, as your heart voices prayer convos to God in your own prayer closet! There, you will discover Him, as well as the real, God-purposed, beloved, amazing you!

HOW TO USE THIS BOOK

Commit to absorb each day's content! Whether a page, a portion, get started! Dive in with expectation to experience God in fresh, new ways and to grasp what's not well known or realized. Day by day, pause, meditate and note new points to glean within each section, and how you are being affected. Pace yourself to see beyond the obvious. Receive every Day's truths, directives and Bible Verses. By prayer, with eyes opened wide and heart available, you will perceive so much more!

Take Notes. Whatever is not yet clear, seek God for fresh understanding, wisdom and knowledge. Read, and re-read, to spotlight a 'new' to know, grasp, absorb and internalize.

Be Intentional to receive. Enjoy God's Word to you! It's like a new friendship, so there's lots to discover. More truth opens as your reach for God is motivated by your faith and love for Him, and your appreciation of who He has made you to be.

Expect, as you explore the proponents of what's unlimited: A better you ~ growing, evolving, emerging with a stronger, deepening faith! Allow God's entry into all your life! You'll begin seeing His 'Views' clearing your spiritual vision. Every facet of His truths will affect every area of ALL things you.

Purpose To Be: A Friend of God, A Truth Seeker (He Is Truth), A Believable Believer with contagious faith, A Student of God's Word, A Witness to and Wielder of His power, An Heir to all His Promises, and A Knower of His Constant Wonders and Grace!

PRAYER...

THE PURSUIT OF

AND PASSAGEWAY TO

THE ONLY LIVING GOD

WHO IS **ALWAYS**

WILLING, AVAILABLE

AND MORE THAN ABLE

TO HELP YOU!

BEHOLD!

"For I know the thoughts and plans that I have
for you, says the Lord, thoughts and plans
for welfare and peace and not for evil,
to give you a future and a hope."
Jeremiah 29:11

"I will cry out to God Most High, to God,
Who performs all things for me."
Psalm 57:2

"I love the Lord because He heard my voice..."
Psalm 116:1

"For as the rain comes down, and the snow from
heaven and do not return there, but water the
earth, and make it bring forth and bud, that it may
give seed to the sower and bread to the eater, so
shall My word be that goes forth from My mouth.
It shall not return to Me void, but it shall
accomplish what I please, and it shall
prosper in the thing for which I sent it."
Isaiah 55:10-11

PEOPLE NEVER GET
THEIR FEELINGS OR THEIR EYES
HURT LOOKING ON THE
BRIGHT SIDE OF THINGS!

PRAYER

GIFTS STABILITY AND CONFIDENCE
TO HAVE SOUL PEACE
AND INNER VISION!

MONDAYS

GOD! He's kinda, sorta, a little bit like aerobics!
As soon as you begin, that is, commit to 'work it',
there are benefits that also begin to slowly grow
even though you can't really see them. It might
be a challenge *if* you're not quite 'O yeah!', yet.

But *if* you keep at it, pressing, striving, diligently
remaining in pursuit while adding to your efforts
a healthy diet, like a daily consumption of God's
Word - the Bread of Life, you'll lose the excesses
of unnecessaries! And, you'll gain much greater
strengths to follow every instruction needed to
increase your supernatural, spiritual shape from
the crown of your head to the 'soul' of your feet.

One of so many and marvelous benefits of God's
Bread is, it won't fill you out. Its beautiful truth -
it fills you in while it's filling you up to the fullest
measures for *your* body, life, and future!

Let God be your Trainer! He gave you potentials,
abilities, capacities, and all you will need, for He
made you to be exceptional, and very strong!

CONFESSION. . .

My relationship with God will affect every relationship in my life. My commitment to growing
closer to God will develop greater, better and
deeper depths of capacities within me.

As I diligently seek God, He will gift me with His
presence and His presents of grace to help me,
to bless me and my life, my labors and efforts,
and to affect others in and through my life.

While I am becoming more of an intimate friend
of God, I am emerging to be stable, trustworthy,
and well able. While I am trusting and requiring
God as a vital need in my life, I am being trans-
formed, renewed, equipped, and refined to be
more loving to God, to myself, and to others.

RE - SOLUTION. . .

I Resolve: To reflect God, and to know Him
in a new, personal relationship.

To know who He made me to be
in my life, and for my purpose.

HEARS A W o r d . . .

To have a nice day, a great life and good success as your goal, purpose and focus are imperatives! And with God's help, you can adjust your sights to have them all!

A new, fresh move of the Spirit is now! To own your part means being more purpose oriented than goal driven. In other words, consider the intent of the result and the process of achieving it rather than only the end result.

An integral part of this is *to be aware* of the import of the means by which you accomplish your results. To be clear, not only thinking about *what* you do, but how you do it, along with the reason or motive behind the *what* you do. It is also wise to take into account the glory God desires by allowing and enabling you to do all you do. And note well, in the grand scheme of things, God IS The Director, with His plans and purposes for all His kids' shows!

Focusing allows you to see the vision. It's greatly needed to grasp the significance of your purposed part in God's Scripts, leads and directives. You are 'gifted' *by the Giver* for a reason, a purpose - AKA *His purpose*: To Reveal God in *your life*, and *all you do*. By His design, you're called to draw others to God, His love and His power. Results will occur, but the processing of purpose and focus is of actual and very significant relevance.

Whether you're a ballerina or a brain surgeon, what you do, or the gift of your talents, is not all you are. Beyond the display and the wrappings is a work in progress. You are not *only* a dancer, or a doctor. You are His, and here for a purpose, also His. That purpose, or assignment, for which you have been created and gifted, isn't just vital, but it must also be recognized and prioritized.

If you look at that gift or job, that situation, or you only, your focus is off point. Improper, out of focus perspectives diminish the whole worth and intent by distorting the vision, along with your part in and of the vision.

When distracted from purpose, you may fail to take hold of the full measure and depth of God's given assignment. To get lost in the glow-ry of the moment by what's called a 'shiny dime' mentality, is to become enamored with the sparkle of a mere coin only to miss the real wealth that is purposed for you. The complete blessing isn't manifested, nor realized. But focus will enable you to see, and in depth, the true worth of the blessing *if* you are discerning, disciplined, and fearlessly patient to wait for it.

KNOW within your purpose is solution, hope, help, and a clear vision for you and others. Beyond you, your goals, gifts and blessings, is the same for others you are yet to meet. The picture is BIG! It's not only you in it! A 360°, panoramic view, will distinctly, and completely reveal 'the' point of purpose that is God's intention for you!

FOCUS on this new page of time with new eyes of faith. It's worth the chance, the opportunity to achieve *above* your reach, and to grab hold of an immeasurably higher, and massively greater mountain top!

CLARITY increases with each step of your climb. Believe God to expand your capacities to see, to do, and to be. If you repeat an old M.O., an out-dated or familiar mode of operating, your efforts may be ineffective. It helps to re-call, "There is a way that *seems* right..." - Proverbs 14:12.

KNOW God *wants* to help you do super-abundantly more than you could ever imagine or think, hope, pray or 'goal'. God made you deliberately and purposely to do exploits, NOT stalk results. He waits patiently only because He so loves you, and He IS God. In fact, He Is SO God!

CHOOSE to make today your day of purpose - to focus in-tentionally *on purpose*! God is willing and able to affect every good work in you *IF* you're willing and available. All your goals can be achieved when you focus. Visualize it - SEE the Big Picture of *You and Your Purpose Manifest!*

REMEMBER, look forward *in your mind* to know and com-prehend the purpose God crafted for your utmost self. . . *Becoming The Greatest Display* Of All You Were Born To Be and Do So God Is Seen! For God's Sake And His Glory, Let Your Purpose Shine To Light Your Paths FORWARD!

PRESS IN...
    To focus and to see the vision.

PRESS THROUGH...
    The process to achieve it.

PRESS ON...
    To reveal God's purpose within you.

BEYOND OPINIONS

One of the best reasons to know God is,
when you have a problem, it's easier to call
someone you do know than someone you don't.

Important decisions require God's consult.

LIfe's storms are for our perfecting, correcting,
refining, learning, changing, and growing.
Who knew pain had a purpose?

A wrong mindset can be as detrimental
as a bad habit, or driving blind.

Bitterness and unforgiveness malfunction
the body like kryptonite disabled Superman.

Every promise of God has a condition but one:
His promise to love you is forever unconditional.

Prayer sends God after your enemies to help you
grow past distractions, and draw closer to Him.

The only way to come out from the struggle
of your darkness is to come up and stand
in the Light of God's Power and Grace!

To focus is to *commit* to your purpose.

Let God be your Chauffeur! He knows where you've got to go, and how to get you there.

If you want your fears quenched, be faith drenched and Word of God entrenched.

Relevant information that is truth may well become transforming revelation.

The discomfort of discipline is far less than the pain of continual regret.

Remember: The devil isn't that big if he can fit under your feet.

Gratitude is a heart condition.

God waits for you to wait on Him.

If you pray about everything, you won't have to worry about anything.

Be who God made you to be more and more, because no one can be you more than you!

Prayer is giving God the whole matter - the purse, the contents, and the straps.

God knew everything about you before you knew Him at all!

God is never surprised because
He is the Onliest Legit Know-It-All!

Reach for long-term aims by refusing
temporary or immediate gratifications.

The more you yield, the more you yield.

The world promotes a proclivity towards
vanity which can produce weaknesses.
God exalts a spirit of humility which
always produces lasting strengths.

IF you are *willing to listen*, God will speak past
your natural hearing, into the depths of your
soul, to answer what you haven't asked yet!

Be a Light bearer rather than a tale teller.

Never stress or worry or fret over what
someone does or doesn't do. Just be sure
you've got oil in *your* lamp (Matthew 25:1-13).

Real forgiveness mends the mind of the
memory, heals the heart of the hurt, and
clears up the eyes to see with compassion.

We are to walk in the supernatural naturally.

PRAY - Daily and nightly!

JESUS!
HE IS THE LORD OF MY LIFE

Jesus Is the Lord of my life
He has done great things for me
Sometimes He was my only friend
He's been my Father, for I was fatherless
When I was weak He healed me with strength
He made me laugh in the midst of madness
He gave me peace I never, ever knew
He gave me life to give me hope and all I need
Jesus! He Is the Lord of my life!

Through every storm He has been my safety
He answers every time I call His Name
He was my shelter when I had no place to go
He has silenced my every fear
I do not understand why or how He loves me
But I know He does
For He keeps me day and night
His Word speaks of His care for me
And I am glad beyond all measure
Jesus Is the Lord of my life!

He Is the only Way, He Is Truth, and He Is Life
He Is more God than I ever imagined
His mercies are tender, fresh and constant.

I was extremely blind
But He made me see everything clearly
I love Him, I need Him so very much
Yes, Jesus
He Is the Lord of my life!

When I asked Him to be in my heart
And to invade my everything
He changed me and my whole world
He rearranged my circumstances
He turned me around
He brought me to real, true life
He taught me what
I never thought to know.

I thank my God, my Jesus
Because He rescued me
He saved me and my future
From my past.

Jesus Is the Lord!
His joy is my strong confidence
His love is my comforting song
For He Is the Lord of my life!

PROMISES
Or Reasons To Like God Even Though
You May Have Trouble Believing In Him!

"The Lord Himself goes before you and will be
with you; He will never leave you nor forsake you.
Do not be afraid, do not be discouraged."
Deuteronomy 31:8

"He shall deliver you in six troubles, yes,
in seven no evil shall touch you."
Job 5:19

"He will not allow your foot to slip or fall!
He Who keeps you will never sleep. The Lord
will keep your going out and your coming in
from this time forth and forevermore."
Psalm 121:3, 8

"Fear of man will prove to be a snare,
but whoever trusts in the Lord is kept safe."
Proverbs 29:25

"I have told you these things, so that in Me
you may have perfect peace and confidence.
In the world you have tribulation, trials, distress,
frustration; but be of good cheer, take courage,
be confident, certain and undaunted! For I have
overcome the world. I have deprived it of power
to harm you, and I have conquered it *for you*."
John 16:33

"Cast all your cares and worries on Him, because
He's always thinking about you and watching
over everything that concerns you."
1 Peter 5:7

Selah!

COMMIT To BELIEVE, KNOW & TRUST God's Word!
God Is Speaking <u>To You Personally</u>. Read, Declare,
Then Apply His Text Messages To Your Life,
Situations, Challenges, Actions & Aspirations.

TAKE NOTES: HOW Will These Verses Affect Me & My Life?

_____

_____

_____

_____

_____

_____

_____

_____

I Must Challenge
My Desire & Pursuit After God
To Greater Levels Of Relationship. . .

The Bible says we are to be 'childlike' (Matthew 18:3). Some folk use this verse to excuse their childish ways. We need to grow up in God to truly appreciate Him, to fully know and taste of His goodness. We crave chips and hot dogs when prime rib and tofu, baked potatoes and fresh veggies are His fare! We settle on the lesser things of God, major in the minors, all while wading in the shallow end of the pool of Living Water.

God is far greater! And what's also exciting, He's available and accessible! The question is: Are we available and accessible to Him? Are we up for more God? Do we really *want* Him? Are we seeking Him diligently?

Reaping a harvest comes only after sowing seeds. Surprisingly, many people think it's okay to receive, taking more and more, without investing or giving back at all. Yet they cry with complaint, like a 'yelp' low score, if their requests and asks aren't a 'next-day' delivery.

But to really get more God and His benefits, God's got to get more you, as in *your* time and attention, prayer convos, worship, and pursuit of Him. Yet, somehow we amnesia-fy this essential of our godly behavior.

God is NOT a religion. He's all about, and He desires, re-lationship! He loves you so much. He'd love to like you, too, but how can He if you're seldom available? And if or when you are, it's because you're hurting, in trouble or a major mess. What kind of friend is that? User, maybe? Or that somebody *you* might avoid hangin' with.

Real spiritual maturation comes only by genuine satura-tion in God. Deep calls to deep. Going beyond the sur-face to the much deeper levels of any right relationship is a vital necessity if there's to be a relationship at all.

To be more of <u>all</u> you can be, you will *so need* more God! Though God doesn't need you, He *wants* you, and wants to give you hope and a future. His desire is for you to al-so want Him. If you are absent, you'll miss His presence and His presents. In truth, you know you need both!

Time out! Take a God break. Run to Him to grow in Him. You'll NEVER be disappointed, rejected, embarrassed, or ever ashamed. Jesus chose you! He got slain to gift you an all-access pass to Himself, and *everything He has*!

God is a wonderful Father Who loves His kids to call Him Abba, Daddy! Why resist His hugs, or the tenderness of His heart. You'll grow and glow from His radiant counte-nance shining over you, and on your whole life. His love is a FOREVER Promise to you, and His Greatest Grace!

THE MIND <u>MUST</u> BE RENEWED TO REMEMBER. . .

Matthew 5:13	I am the salt of the earth.
John 1:12	I am a child of God.
Acts 1:8	I am a witness of Christ.
1 Peter 1:3	I am born again.

THEREFORE. . .

> I <u>am</u> significant, accepted and secure in God, and through God, I <u>am</u> able to do all things!

SUGGESTED CRITICAL READING. . .

The Word of God ~ the Bible (Basic Instructions Before Leaving Earth), is the manual to function in life, and to grow through its challenges. We can't leave home or have a successful home without it.

Practically every life scenario or condition is related to within its pages. The solutions, remedies, wisdoms we need are written by God, our Savior Friend, Who always desires the very best for us. It's fully predicated on His intense love for us! It is a *must daily read* to stay well, to live wholly alive, and to keep the evil one at bay.

Begin with Genesis, or John's Gospel. Foundational and historical, they background God's Covenant with us, as well as His plan for all mankind. Learn, enjoy His Story to discover His unfathomable love for you!

COURAGE DOES NOT ALWAYS ROAR.
SOMETIMES COURAGE IS THE QUIET VOICE
AT THE END OF THE DAY SAYING,
"I WILL TRY AGAIN TOMORROW."

MARY ANNE RADMACKER

"BE STRONG AND OF GOOD COURAGE. . ."

JOSHUA 1:6A

PRAYER BIRTHS COURAGE!

Prayers & Concerns

_____

_____

_____

_____

_____

_____

_____

_____

_____

_____

_____

_____

Observations & Revelations

_____

_____

_____

_____

_____

_____

_____

_____

_____

_____

_____

_____

_____

Hopes & Intentions

_____

_____

_____

_____

_____

_____

_____

_____

_____

_____

_____

_____

_____

Gratitude Declarations

_____

_____

_____

_____

_____

_____

_____

_____

_____

_____

_____

_____

DARE...

To Reach Out And Touch

G O D With ALL Your Heart!

Begin With PRAYER...

It Gets His Full Attention!

TUESDAYS

To Praise God... is a little bit like unto the care or cleaning of a throw rug! Shake it, beat it, slap it... and the more you do, the cleaner and the better it gets, and the more debris free it becomes.

And so, likewise, is our praise to God! With each exuberant shout, enthusiastic passion expressed, with every clap of our hands, we birth new views of God and fresh freedoms from those annoying harassments the ol' enemy of our soul adamantly imposes upon us. We know them too well - anger, insecurities, fear, depression, doubts, frustration, anxiety... all distractions and disruptors of peace.

But the more we praise the Lord, the more we will reset our focus, and grow in resistance. Much like teflon coating on cookware protects it from stains or foods sticking to it, our shouts build up defiant barriers as walls of defense. Our shouts double in effect as invitations for the Presence of God, our Shield and Protector, Who inhabits praisings with His graciousness, extending His peace like a river of provision over us - like a covered, hidden city!

So let us make a joyful, loud, exhilarating, shaking and slapping lots of tambourines - with thundery clapping hands, exciting noise unto the Lord!

~ Psalm 100:1

35

CONFESSION. . .

God is in love with me.

God wants to talk to me, and with me.

God is watching over me, not spying on me.

RE - SOLUTION

I Resolve: To seek God's ways, Word, plans
and counsel continually.

To praise God in all thing more.

To relax in God's love more.

To nurture my spirit more.

To listen more objectively.

To pray for others more.

HEARS A Word...

Love! Is it just another four letter word? Has it become a 'delete' on your to-do-list? Why does love have such connotations as 'Uh, NO!', dread, 'don't get involved', or lust? The world, the flesh and the devil do a fine job of perverting what is the greatest gift.

The well known, heralded verse of Scripture that tells of God's heart for all humanity states - "God *so loved* the world that He gave His only begotten Son, that *whoever* believes in Him will have eternal life" - John 3:16. Smart or not, down and out, rich or poor, anyone can own this outrageous gift *by believing*! Our 'thanks' would be giving that love back to God and others, to family, friends, and humanity! What a bargain for such a tremendously great and *free* gift, besides being an amazing grace!

But in so many places, love is missing! At work, home, in the church - the building and Body of Christ, discord and strife, or other not-at-all-nice attitudes and behaviors distract. Why can't we agree to get along? Where *is* the love? Anybody got any compassion?

As a result, the tender aspects of God's love are clearly not perceived. This is likely why, and too often, traces of His love are a failed expectation. Sadly, without being expressed, love is not given its holy significance, or allowed its power to heal hearts, and present peace.

Still, God, by His graciousness, always leans in to help us understand, to take hold of His outreached hand of precious love. But the only way we *capture* what is in His hand, and grasp His concepts, mind and ways, is to LET GO of *whatever* we tightly hold onto. It cannot be stressed enough: *Letting go* gives entry to God's love in our lives! Why hold flawed excuses that are greatly contrary to living life when God IS The Greatest Love? He IS worth our acceptance, our gratitude, and giving our love back to Him in return. Shall we *let go* to bless God, or expect Him to bless our mess?

Why take the less-thans when every cost of life giving love has been 'paid in full'? You'll only get to know, to feel how good and real it is IF you *choose* to accept it! God will never force you to love Him, to be blessed, or to believe Him. It is a CHOICE to wisely choose!

Who's loving you unconditionally lately or ever? Rich, poor, good or bad, happy, sad or mad, His love is real, and forever *for you*! His love is a Gift that comes with another Gift - Himself! This God, Creator of universes, wants to be <u>with you</u>, in your life now, and for always! What a concept, especially if you have ever felt like you didn't want to be with you yourself!

God is kind, patient, so generous. His love is a forever always, tenderhearted love that's a unique expression of a compassion we will never merit nor deserve. Just imagine, as God woos us to Himself, He's *still* loving us in all our unlovely ways, stages, bad hair days, or hostilities showing up as mood swings. That's greater love than we know how to contain. That's exactly why it is forever!

By His Word, His Love Letter, He beckons us to the next step, to the next level of our growth in Him and our lives. Plus, He promises good success and His wisdom to prosper us 'if' we believe, receive and follow all His leadings (Joshua 1:8). When we do, another benefit is graced... God will watch over *all* our concerns, and *all* things us!

That love you're searching for only comes from God. His love is a teacher, enabling you to love well whether it be God, yourself, or others. Going to the Source of it all, for sure, is always the best practice.

God may express His love through a person or situation. However He cleverly manifests it, that display says He IS good, and He IS love. Know, He's been in love with you for a very long time - before you ever knew His Name!

What God gives you is Grace He desires you to give away, to share, so someone else gets a glimpse, a taste, a touch of His *for real* love! Let somebody know of your amazing God! His kind of love only increases in depth and passion of heart. Certainly, it is far too grand in its capacities not to share. It is a love to be received in its immeasurable expressions, and never, not ever to be unrequited!

BEYOND OPINIONS

Follow after God with fresh eyes,
and without previous perceptions.

You've come a very long way
when God's will is your only option.

BE a witness for God by your behavior!
Aim to let Him be seen when you are.

You cannot want more for others
than they want for themselves.

Unforgiveness can produce disabling
diseases, cancers, haltings, and death.
Forgiveness is a life producer to every
forgiver, and new hope to the forgiven.

Never diet when it comes to God!
Psalm 34:8 is an irresistible invite:
"O taste and see that God Is Good!"

Are you impressing, or impacting?

Life is like a record, or a CD.
The key to its fullest enjoyment is
to avoid getting stuck in those grooves.

God has a beautiful human side ~ Jesus!

To wait on God is to plant time in fertile Ground.

Confess your love for God when you praise Him!
You will discover the One Who first loved you!

Come to God, just as you are, to become who He
made you to be ~ the YOU you've never been.

Spiritual synergy happens when we co-operate,
co-labor, submit, obey and agree with God.

Praise produces bumper crops, but murmuring
creates stops after stops after stops.

Personalize and apply God's Word in all your life.
It works like sunscreen - to filter out those ultra
violent ways that can be extremely damaging,
not to mention unsafe, and life-threatening.

As believers, we're not any better, just better off.
It's not that we are worthy, but we have worth.
It's only because we *are* God's own children.

Trying to 'Find Yourself'? Just ask God to help,
because He always knows where you are.

Don't let it bother you when you speak truth
and people don't believe you. Many don't
believe Jesus, or know He IS The Truth.

The enemy distracts you to subtract from you.

DECIDE to evolve from mediocrity to own the disciplines of excellence and exceptionalism.

When trouble comes, we come close to God. But, why wait?

In *going for it*, be sure you're going forward.

The mind elevated above the Spirit can be a snare to one's life, purpose and destiny.

Remember to represent God, not just you.

Proof of repentance is changed behavior.

Lots of things are true,
but they may not be the truth.

Stop the preys with your PRAISE!

ESP - Extra Spiritual Perception equips us to better know, hear, learn, see, and grow up.

Jesus hung on the Cross so we can hang on.

Add to your list of urgent, must-do things, saying, "Thank you!" more, and sincerely.

PRAY - To recognize the gain in your pain,
          and to understand, with great pain
          always comes your greatest power.

24 STEP PROGRAM

1. Jesus
2. Lord
3. The Christ
4. Savior
5. Friend
6. Love
7. Truth
8. Help
9. Hope
10. The Holy One
11. Peace
12. Healer
13. Restorer
14. Creator
15. Promise Keeper
16. Almighty
17. The Giver of Life
18. Messiah
19. Miracle Worker
20. Advocate
21. Father, Abba, Daddy
22. First
23. Last
24. The Most High God

PROMISES
From The Original Promise Keeper!

"Be strong and very courageous.
Be not afraid, neither be dismayed,
for the Lord your God is with
you wherever you go."
Joshua 1:9b

"Fear the Lord, you His saints! There is
no lack to those who truly trust and
worship Him with godly fear."
Psalm 34:9

"True humility and respect for the Lord lead
a man to riches, honor and long life."
Proverbs 22:4

"I will restore health to you and heal you
of your wounds, says the Lord, because
they called you an outcast."
Jeremiah 30:17a

"'For I will surely deliver you, and you shall
not fall by the sword, but your life shall be
as a prize to you because you have put
your trust in Me', says the Lord."
Jeremiah 39:18

"The thief comes to steal, kill and destroy.
I have come that you might have life,
and have it more abundantly."
John 10:10

Selah!

COMMIT To BELIEVE, KNOW & TRUST God's Word!
God Is Speaking <u>To You Personally</u>. Read, Declare,
Then Apply His Text Messages To Your Life,
Situations, Challenges, Actions & Aspirations.

TAKE NOTES: HOW Will These Verses Affect Me & My Life?

_____

_____

_____

_____

_____

_____

_____

I CAN BE...

A Loser ~ and shrink from my accountability,
my purpose, and my responsibilities.

An Excuser ~ and live in my coulda, woulda,
shoulda state of mind and mistakes.

An Accuser ~ and blame everything on others,
especially my faults or shortcomings.

A Chooser ~ and embrace my chance at life,
mindfully choosing to follow Christ,
Who Is My Abundant Life Giver.

I Must Challenge
My Love & Passion For God
To Greater Levels Of Commitment...

Examine again, "God so loved the world that He gave..."
- John 3:16. What are we giving to the God we 'so love'
lately? An offering? Some praise? Donations of time,
or a few good cans? Maybe a visit to Church last, uh...
How's $5 to that homeless person instead of the regu-
lar lotto quik-pick? Oh, to God be the glory!

Reality check: Love is an action word. Love acts to declare its existence. Its language speaks of its depths of
mind. A *lover* is, and must be, an expression of, and a
witness to the very defining of its integrity of heart.

Love is incredibly multifaceted, deliberate, passionate,
and constant. The more you become submitted to real
love's ways and means, the more you are fashioned by
its hues of splendor, and limitless expressions of grace.

Love is not always pleasure, but it's a forever treasure.
It never seek itself. It pursues *giving* to state its truth.
As a lover of Jesus, how will you make known your love
for Him? Do you show your love in ways that summon
Him to you, like metal is irresistible to a magnet?

Jesus proved His love and His commitment to us when
He made us His always, forever Passion at His Cross!

Passionately. . .

Reassess... Review... Re-examine... Reconsider...
The How, The Way, And The Why You Love God.

And Then. . .

Remember, Repent, Restore, Rebuild, Re-establish,
Repair, Rekindle, Recapture, Recreate, Reconfirm,
Realize, Refresh, Refine, Renew, Reflect, Relate...
That You May RE-PRESENT Your Heart To God,
    And RE-STATE ALL Your Love For Him!

THE MIND <u>MUST</u> BE RENEWED TO REMEMBER. . .

John 17:23	I am loved by God.
2 Corinthians 6:16	I am God's temple.
Galatians 3:13	I am redeemed.
Colossians 2:10	I am complete in Christ.

THEREFORE. . .

I <u>am</u> important to God Who cares for and about me, and through God, I <u>am</u> becoming my identity.

SUGGESTED CRITICAL READING. . .

Perhaps you've begun browsing through Genesis. If so, or not, continue through Exodus and Deuteronomy for great details of our established Covenant. The Old Testament accounts foreshadow the New Testament fulfillments of God's Promises, and the freedoms The Blood of Christ *still grants* to all who would dare believe.

Examine God's Word in light of diet and health. Exodus tells of Israel's just-enough-manna-for-today mandate to speak fresh perspectives regarding food intake, and our appetites. Often we think of hunger in the physical sense when it may be a spiritual issue. To be filled with God's Spirit is, in fact, our mandated food today!

Remember, God is craving you! When you hunger for Him, you will arrive *to know* He alone satisfies.

Prayers & Concerns

_____

_____

_____

_____

_____

_____

_____

_____

_____

_____

_____

_____

Observations & Revelations

_____

_____

_____

_____

_____

_____

_____

_____

_____

_____

_____

_____

_____

Hopes & Intentions

_____

_____

_____

_____

_____

_____

_____

_____

_____

_____

_____

_____

Gratitude Declarations

_____

_____

_____

_____

_____

_____

_____

_____

_____

_____

_____

_____

_____

HOPE YOURSELF UP FROM

D
O
W
N!

WHILE YOU'RE DOWN THERE,

TRY P R A Y E R ~

IT'S THE UP ELEVATOR!

WEDNESDAYS

Listening to God is sorta like listening to the radio. First, you've got to plug in to the power source to enable your radio to work. Getting the dial finely tuned on the right station is key for clearer reception, because you don't want to miss a Word!

At times, you'll need to turn up the volume when static or noise occurs, and drowns out the sound. It's *necessary* to avoid interferences that disturb you from listening, but of greater importance, distract you from hearing what's spoken to you.

God's got a great program planned for a great audience - that would be you! Be assured, it's amazingly informative. It details how blessed He wants you to be by simply following His for-such-a-time-as-this broadcasts, learning all about Him and His ways, discovering His incredible powers, and too, the heartfelt delight it is to Him for you to tune-in regularly! F.Y.I., He wrote all of it - creating every Passage, Chapter and Verse of His Word, with the passion of His love, *just for you*!

You'll want to always listen in to God's fabulously phenomenal All-Things-Are-Possible Network. It's your daily Truth and Power Good News God-Cast!

CONFESSION. . .

I will go forward and possess what God has
for me. I will walk in who I am. I believe in
God, and I trust all that He speaks to me.

I am ready - with great expectation, for my
transformation. I will pray for and through
all my growth and development processes.

I am determined to wear my joy, and with a
smile, as both are acts of shining witness
to my strengths, and stalwart weapons
to smite the enemy with confusion.

For all things and in all things I will give God
thanks and praise, especially if I struggle to
feel like it, or when it sounds crazy to do so.

I WILL BE A Radical Witness!

RE - SOLUTION. . .

I Resolve: To be a better steward over all
my portions: life, time, health,
diet, rest, words, wealth, faith
walk, behavior, relationships.

HEARS A Word...

Do you look or feel like *the worst* sometimes? Or do you look and feel great, like *alive*, ever? Think about it! What will you be wearing this Spring, Fall, or this Wednesday? Will it be A) Your new, done-with-what-*'was-done'* outfit, with an Abundant Life Logo on the label? Or B) Your old, lyin'-to-ya-&-on-ya, so uncool *grave clothes* from those yester-life's seasons of struggle? Let's chat!

This 'visual' gripped me like a vise when I read of Lazarus getting raised from the dead! Jesus spoke, 'Come forth!', while Laz was *still in the grave*, wrapped in his wardrobe of binding grave clothes (John 11:43). Come-pelling!

The vivid reality of 'grave clothes' loomed out at me like a personal threat. 'Wow!' was on my lips as I heard in my heart the Lord say, "Many of My people wear them." My 'Wow!' attached to a feeling of woe. Whoa! That is not a lively, lovely, nor any way a brand fashion statement!

Jesus called Lazarus out from his grave, but he had to be 'set free' from the bandages of death's bondage. A great call, and a clear picture! So *what* are we wearing? Do we dress for death? Isn't it for life we live? How can we get to progress mode if grave clothes are *still* a dress code? Surely, bondage will never be a life support system, nor an accessory to living in the truth of real freedom. It will mean taking off 'what was', to wear 'what's now' ~ LIFE!

For certain, it will be difficult to breathe and be all that, to look good and en vogue, wrapped head to toe in binding limitations. (Is this how the layered look started?!?) Life limiters - the past, anger, hurts, guilt, negativity, unforgiveness, and shame, are ALL robbers! They *cannot* equip us to live a life that's absolutely alive and set free! Shall we disrobe from the hot mess of binding bondage?

Question 2: Ever wonder why it's easy to slip into something comfy? It's familiar! You know it by heart. It's like those aforementioned life robbers we got saved from to only revisit when we're in pain and not sure what else to do. But God has mercies of great escapes from the robberies of our freedom, and the challenges we encounter *when we do not listen* to hear God's call like dead (I said DEAD!) Lazarus did! The Lord God, Who loves us, sent His Word to rescue us, people (Psalm 107:20)!

Lazarus wore grave clothes until Jesus commanded: BE Set Free from them. This same Word - *Be Set Free*, is for all our life! God's Word of Power is still alive *NOW!* WE can partake of His Wonders *any time* we want a fresh, 'I am alive!' look. His Word is the mirror we *need* to know and see His Truth. It's The Way and How to rise up from *the worst,* to look and be as God Is - *Greatly Alive!*

Scripture tells us if anyone 'Be In Christ', that person is a brand new being. Old, *dead stuff* is gone! Fresh and new are *ready-to-wear* NOW (2 Corinthians 5:17)! YAY!

REFUSE to be bound by *the worst* of any guilt, shame, or pain of teary, ugly cries - ALL bondage. Such 'styles' are far from becoming. For maybe the first, and for sure, the last time, lay ALL *the worst* of those whatevers down at the foot of the cross! Or, how 'bout in the trash?!

REALIZE, as a believer, you're <u>not</u> better than others, but better off! It is not that you're worthy, but *of worth*. It is not about being 'all that', but becoming much more than ever. Why? Because that God Guy, Jesus, so loves you!! His love impassioned Him to get nailed on a cross to land you the rights to be abundantly alive, absolutely whole, plus completely unbound and set free. Oh Yeah, YES!

RECOGNIZE, we all got more than a measure of *the worst* grief. We all got rejected, disrespected, abased, abused, accused, bruised. We wandered in wildernesses, beat up and down, cut and stripped. Yes, we suffered. But now, <u>we got JESUS</u>, Who tasted each one of those nightmares, *and death*! He came out ALIVE, leaving His grave clothes behind, so that we can too! He went forth to live A REAL, TRUE LIFE, so that YOU CAN TOO (John 20:6-9)!

If you change your clothes, if you change your mind, you *will change your life*. Don't you want a new outfit? How 'bout a brand new wardrobe to match your new life? As with Lazarus, it starts by *hearing* God's call out from the bandages of every bondage to dead, NO LIFE things!

That'll clearly mean: NO MORE grave clothes! BRAVE it! God can and will give you a makeover so you're enabled to rise over ALL opponents to your life, ALL by His grace and power. You'll start looking like Him to be done with looking and feeling like *the worst*, with its NOT cool, re-curring taunts of the 'what was done' priors!

It's up to you! What do you want to wear? How will you want to look? Why wait to improve when all you need is already gifted to you, *and paid for*! A resurrection, a re-direction can both be yours. Simply answer the call out from *every encumbrance* preventing your for REAL life! This is Choose Life Day! God said: "Choose ye this day!" - Joshua 24:15. It's time: *(Your Name)* , "Come Forth!"

You only need to trust God Who IS trustworthy, and He's an Incredible Designer! (Take a look at the universe!) He will make you look good, feel good and be good, too! So, why not step out, over those binding rags? They did not fit nor ever look good on you! Besides, don't you wanna be 'alive' and in color, wearing your fancy dancin' shoes?

Get your best brave on! It's time! Choose to be set-like-a-flint-determined to ratchet up, and DO it! You're 'bout to be, look and feel like the winner you were designed by God to *Always Be*! ARISE! 'COME FORTH!', In The Most Loving, Magnificently Alive, Beautiful Name Of Jesus!!!

BEYOND OPINIONS

Like your I.D., protect your peace.

FOCUS! Keep walking forward, and
far past what things are not your tasks.

Greed is taking what you want, or think
you'll need, without giving anything back.

Eliminate mindsets devoid of appreciation.

It is much too late to *only* be Black or White,
Red, Yellow, or Brown, Female, Male, or
Child. We MUST Be His - The Lord's.

The pain of your circumstances is a reminder
that the joy of your blessing is next.

The greatest fear of the enemy is you *knowing
and believing* who you are, and Whose you are.

Correction is your GPS ~ God's Purpose Saver.

Is Christ-ianity or Church-ianity your center?

Once you know the vast measures of God,
you'll find all things as being very small.

Talent is a gift, but integrity if a choice.

You are a vessel bought with a price.
Your purpose is to be filled with God and His
benefits so that you will BE His Overflowing Well
from which others - the lame, the blind and deaf,
the creeps, the discouraged and sick, as well, the
dead to life ~ can draw God's Abundant Life from
the Rivers of Living Water within you - John 7:38.
Unless you share Him, pouring Him into their dry,
lifeless, contrary places, how will they get know?
The question is: How much Jesus do you have?
PRAY to have so much more of GOD to share!

Outside of sports or contests, we were never
called to compare or compete with each other.
The Standard and Example of Measure is Christ.

Never limit God to what you have in mind, how
you feel, nor what you've learned or yet assume.

Take a rest to be enabled to take on the rest.

Your anointing does NOT exempt you from
accountability, order, or regard for others.

Too often we look past each other
instead of looking past our faults.

Prayer is the bridge from the natural
to the supernatural, from the probable
and possible to the absolutely impossible.

CAN I GET A WITNESS?

As a believer with zeal and ardor for God, and a directive to share all that with the world, one might find herself, or himself, with an unction to urge others to 'come into The Light'! O, but oft, however, there's a tendency, like a flaw in the ol' flesh, to lean toward being a Light filter.

Our purpose is to turn people <u>on</u> to His Light - like a Light switch! Staying in the 'on' position allows God's Light to fully flood the atmosphere and dispel any darkness.

Blindly, and unwisely, we prompt others to 'see the Light' through the filter of our views and revelations, or our versioned interpretations of truth. What's worse, we'll open the miry screen of our past and its variegations. That results in 'filtering' what they may need to hear and see, or come to learn and know, in the absolute Light of Truth.

Our understanding, concept or sway could be a veneer of logic to someone God wants to take beyond a surface perception. We're in His way if we fill-in the blanks, or screen the brightness of the Light, like a dimmer switch.

Thank God He allows partnership in His plans to share His Truth, but we must avoid managing His business. We 'get' to be a part! It's all God's show even if we 'solo' now and again. Learning to be still, knowing He IS very well able, *and God*, is due humility. By grace, He trusts us with all we have or do, and in every given opportunity.

We only need to be committed and willing to decrease. God will then increase the effectiveness of our efforts, our witness, and the yielding of our earnestly obedient, selfless, motive-free - like a servant, labors of service!

Our job is God's Light bearing messenger. We are never to mess with or mess up the privilege of bringing to display His Light Show. Imagine Archangel Gabe ad-libbing Mary's message to proclaim his version! Impeccable integrity stands, for it is praiseworthy. We all so need the same kind of honesty to acknowledge, honor and please our God. We *should* desire Christ's mind and servant's heart to enable our followship of His leadings as we surrender, with utmost reverence, to serve Him.

Why not dismiss the 'control' tendency anchored in our flesh? To exercise our authority is to *command* order in our lives. We are given this power by Jesus Christ, Who has ALL power and authority (Luke 10:19).

When we do get to share our faith in God, His anointing of excellence enables us. When we voice testimonies of God, His empowerment visibly manifests! Our faultless witness and committed hearts remain, with much more brilliance than the ploys of anyone's 'selfie'-ways, and dull, unenlightening 'dis'-course! O SHINE, Jesus!

PROMISES
Or Reasons To Trust God Anyway!

"The words and promises of the Lord are
pure words, like silver refined in an earthen
furnace, purified seven times over."
Psalm 12:6

"The Lord is my light and my salvation, whom
shall I fear? The Lord is the strength of my life,
of whom shall I be afraid? When evil men came
to destroy me, they stumbled and fell!"
Psalm 27:1-2

"Oh, taste and see that the Lord is good!
How blessed is the one who trusts
and takes refuge in Him."
Psalm 34:8

"Who is like the Lord our God, Who dwells on high,
Who humbles Himself to consider the things in
the heavens and in the earth? He raises up
the poor out of the dust and lifts the needy out
of the ash heap, that He may seat him with
princes - even the princes of His people."
Psalm 113:5-8

"You will keep him in perfect peace whose mind
is stayed on You, because he trusts in You."
Isaiah 26:3

"A bruised reed He will not break, and a
dimly burning wick He will not quench;
He will bring forth justice in truth."
Isaiah 42:3

Selah!

COMMIT To BELIEVE, KNOW & TRUST God's Word!
God Is Speaking To You Personally. Read, Declare,
Then Apply His Text Messages To Your Life,
Situations, Challenges, Actions & Aspirations.

TAKE NOTES: HOW Will These Verses Affect Me & My Life?

_____

_____

_____

_____

_____

_____

_____

I Must Challenge
My Commitment To God
By Greater Levels Of Service. . .

The Bible tells us, Jesus, King of kings, and Lord of lords, came to planet earth to serve. Hmmm. A huge question to ask is, 'Why do so many of us *demand* service?'

Two principles of Scripture are clear. First, as believers and followers of Christ, vs. me-myself-&-I, are we not to be His examples of 'less self' (Matthew 16:24)? Second, "While the earth remains..." seed time and harvest prevail (Genesis 8:22). So clearly, sowing precedes reaping! So why the serve-me-give-me mood swing? We know (?), or should recall, God gave BIG! So then, shouldn't we?

Some folks may think they're *so* anointed that the oil on their lives will leak out to be snatched up by the people, or the floor! But the oil is *given to be poured out* on the ones served, like the captives or oppressed, the abused, helpless or hopeless, and every whosoever. That oil is not to be withheld, but freely given - just as Jesus is.

Our misinterpretations prevent God's anointing, His gift, reducing it to our 'annoyings'. We neglect the center of our faith: God and His love! To win people to the Lord, inviting them to taste of His goodness, to know Him and experience His power, instead of all our 'us'-nesses, our every effort's proof *must be love.*

That love is an action! It is seldom silent, nor dormant. It intentionally manifests. It is ever active, sharing its strengths and abilities, especially in the face of its recipients' weaknesses, vulnerabilities, their fears, need or pain. That's because love is a *constant giver*.

Love is a yielded servant. To possess it leads to serving. Like the love of a doting father, not enough can be done for the object of its affection. Such is Father God! He's ever giving, always loving, so completely caring for us.

To be followers of Christ, and to love Him, we will want to be of service. Our desire becomes our 'delight' to be pleasing Him. The Bible confirms, "Delight in God... He will give you the desires of your heart." - Psalm 37:4.

This Verse reveals God will teach us *what* to desire. He will draw the hearts and minds yielded to Him *to desire Him*. By seeking Him more, we get *rewarded* (He IS our Prize!) to know His heart, which helps us experience His Presence more deeply. And with NO demands from our Lord, we will yearn for His ways of doing in all our ways of actions and efforts. As our pursuit grows, we grow to be recipients - vessels containing God, filled with benefits and graces He has forever purposed for us.

What we give will give a return. Harvests are attached! Every gesture of love for God reaps His Love's Graces. We only need *to yield* to receive His Abundant Yield!

What's within us IS God, Of and From God. Our yielded in surrender servant's heart becomes the platter upon which The Living Bread *is served*. No *self* is seen. What we give *IS what He has given*. We then obtain His more *as our increase*. We grow to be so much more, all while we're becoming *as He Is* in the earth (1 John 4:17)!

God's plan is for us to be so blessed by our giving, we'll <u>be</u> the blessing part of the Abrahamic Covenant. We'll *partner* with God to become vessels through which others are blessed by God. Liberated, we liberate, set-free, we set others free. What we're given, we'll *want* to give so that we grow, increase and magnify God's love. And by all this, we magnify God, Who IS Love. It's SO God!

Love for God defined is having a committed, submitted heart willing to serve the One Who 'so loved'. It IS love, it IS giving beyond the call of any duty or obligation. To decrease allows Jesus *to be seen* more (John 3:30). By this exchange, you increase, grow, and produce greater yields that are beyond expectations or imaginings. It is absolutely supernatural! You can't make this up!

And the resulting 'special effects' ~ God's amazing love and tremendous power begin to show up! It all causes you to become God's Anointed Gift, bearing greatly so much oil! How can we *serve Him*? What more can we *do for God*? Let Him count the ways! Hallelujah!

THE MIND <u>MUST</u> BE RENEWED TO REMEMBER. . .

Romans 8:37	I am more than a conquerer.
Ephesians 4:32	I am forgiven.
Ephesians 6:10	I am strong in God.
Colossians 3:12	I am the elect of God.

THEREFORE. . .

I <u>am</u> approved by God, I <u>am</u> settled in God, and by His grace, I <u>am</u> healthy in my body, soul and spirit!

SUGGESTED CRITICAL READING. . .

Proverbs - the Book of Wisdom, awaits to pour refreshing revelation on you, your faith, and your whole life.

There are 31 Chapters, one for each day. Once completed, begin again to glean more of its wisdoms. Each Verse becomes food for thought, principles for life, strengths for your soul, and fuel for your faith's journey.

Add a Psalm or two for super-sized spiritual clout. With all of that, your praise becomes: #1. A tool, to add God's insights that implement all you do, and #2. A weapon, to enable your victory over the enemy on a regular basis!

Read credible authors to contribute to all your pursuits. Seize every opportunity to grow His *greats* within you. It only gets better, stronger, more, and GOD-er!

Give God ALL You've Got Because

He Gave You ALL You Have!

And Know,

The More You PRAY

The More You Will Have To Give!

Prayer Concerns

_____

_____

_____

_____

_____

_____

_____

_____

_____

_____

_____

_____

_____

_____

Observations & Revelations

Hopes & Intentions

_____

_____

_____

_____

_____

_____

_____

_____

_____

_____

_____

_____

Gratitude Declarations

_____

_____

_____

_____

_____

_____

_____

_____

_____

_____

_____

_____

_____

OBEDIENCE IS ALWAYS BEST

THE 1st TIME AROUND!

PRAYER

ALWAYS HELPS ACCOMPLISH

WHAT YOU CANNOT

ON YOUR OWN...

LIKE, FOR EXAMPLE,

CONSISTENT OBEDIENCE!

THURSDAYS

The quality of your life will depend on your availability to access God's ability in every area of your life.

Once the Lord is in every dimension of your ways, means and lifestyle, in each room of your living domain, He will light up the darkness, lighten all loads, and by enlightenment, lessen the lessons you may often repeat.

By His mandate, you will find all your days becoming much brighter. Then, at night, you'll sleep better and more soundly - with refreshings upon your mind and body to meet your new day. All panic, stress, unrest and fears will begin to dissipate, only to disappear!

IF you want a great life, divine power and uncommon favor, give God your ALL-ACCESS Pass to ALL things you!

Take Note:
Only What You Do For Christ Will Last!

REMEMBER. . .

Prioritize - Put God first, then all else will
line up. Set specific times to honor,
worship, and fellowship with God.

Memorialize - Recall things God has done
before. He is the same yesterday,
now, and forever. He can *again*.

Sacrifice - Praise in difficulty or great trial
is sacrificial, as well an offering that
pleases God. Praise will invite His
Presence which brings His favor.

Realize - As a child, friend and servant of
Father God, there is no good thing
He will ever withhold from you.

Maximize - Put time and energy to work in
God ordained, Kingdom-building,
soul-winning life practices.

RE - SOLUTION

I Resolve - To pray about everything.
To praise God in every wait.
To thank God for Who He Is.

HEARS A Word...

A Critical Word Is ~ "Obedience is better than sacrifice."
- 1 Samuel 15:22. I read it, and knew it was 'the' writ for
living a God-tiered life! I instantly said, 'O thanks, God!',
for being so cool, patient, and never yelling at me when
I failed to make that 'O'! And for certain, only One has
ever had a perfect 'O' record. That would be Jesus!

As Christians, we become a new creation of obedience,
developing in righteousness, godly behaviors, love and
other betters. *By God's Grace*, we get freed from every
slavery to that dis-'O' thing which, by the way, ends up
in death! That's because sin's paycheck is a death row
sentence (Romans 6:23), not just another bad day.

Great discoveries are made by seeking God, growing in
Him, and knowing His Word. One vitally important find
for life is the 'obedience factor'. Its wages secure God's
blessings. Another fab fact - *you* decide, *you* choose!
It's a pro-life-or-death thing, and *your* choice!

Jesus said, "If you love Me, *you will obey!*" - John 14:15.
Obedience is the E-Ticket to God's Abundant Life Show!
The Big 'O' Mandated Directive is down payment, the investment into the land of God's promises. His charge to
obey is solely based on the *deposit of Himself* within us!
By the power of His Holy Spirit, God enables us to perform this feat, Hallelujah! (We are NOT in this alone!)

The first step of salvation is faith - belief in God. Next is obeying Him, which 1. Produces a consistent liberty that is a view of Christianity in its most believably compelling form, and 2. Holds us accountable to the debt we so owe Jesus for dying and setting us free from sin's slavery.

Oh, okay! But why do we repeat the same things, or bad behaviors, over and over, apologizing again and again, as we wear out, 'I'm so sorry', professing we're 'so saved!'? It's the flesh and its tendencies to swell up over our eyes and minds. But we can, "Submit to God! Resist the devil so he'll flee..." - James 4:7. What's truth, our *submission* <u>must</u> be at the root of all our efforts of obedience.

Another question of incentive: How long can we make it *without* what God has for us? Our receiving is akin to us giving our 'O's - the sow'n'reap rule, again! Obedience is *the* ingredient to bring it to pass. It's like baking powder! We need it for our cakes to rise, and our souls to ascend.

O Cake! How 'bout we ask God for a change of appetite? It's a natural factor to flesh which longs for what's incongruous to the Spirit. And obedience is not natural. Galatians 5:24-25 tells us to *walk in the Spirit*, the supernatural, so we <u>are able</u> to put under foot our flesh cravings, the natural. That's full-on manifested submission!

The Holy Spirit helps the infirmities of our flesh, its tendencies to err, and iniquities bending our appetites and attentions away from righteousness. Romans 8:26 confirms His help to change our minds, desires, habits, not-so-nice attitudes, and any all-about-me weaknesses.

Obedience - yielding to God, green lights His power within us. We become constituents, partners, effective components of His Grace Distribution Process. Our efforts and His graces *conjoin* to bring salvation to every place in our lives, and to *act* as a holy contagion to others.

Obedience to God *proves* we can be trusted. It forms as it reforms us, growing our character, and anchoring us in His righteousness. While that's underway, what displays is a stewardship of integritous excellence *from the heart.* As we grow, so grows our spirituality in our relationships, credibility, strengths and power as it's flowing over onto our personalities. We then reflect Jesus in a genuine, relatable kinship. Let us thank our Lord Jesus for so much, and so greatly empowering, outrageous love!

REMEMBER: Obedience begins with YOU - in your heart! It becomes *your desire* to please and submit to God, The One you love anyway, right? It is a radical surrender that lands in and on you greater capacities of strengths, with abilities beyond you! It has power to stay you up on your God-Paths of purpose, and in a vibrant, committed bond to God Himself - The Giver of life, and The Lover of your soul! He is extremely SO Worthy of ALL our O's!

BEYOND OPINIONS

You can magnify your problems with worry
and be stressed! Or... You can magnify the
Lord with your praise and be blessed. Duh!

Five great things about your past:
1) It has passed, 2) You made it through,
3) You are still standing, 4) It validated you,
5) These graces prepared you to grow forward.

It's okay to tremble while you trust God!
He will reward you, and give you
a burger with that shake!

Let pride be pried from your heart,
your mind, and all things you.

Faith is not a piece of fine jewelry you
only choose to wear on special occasions.

Get settled in God to avoid settling for less.

Be willing to hear more than your own voice.

Are you *your* version, or God's version of you?

The least you do should <u>always</u> be your best
effort, and that with utmost excellence.

Challenges are allowed by God to build our
faith, confidence, character and integrity
as we grow to trust Him, for God knows
we'll need Him to lift the heavy stuff.

Vision is the vehicle to your dreams.
You just need to focus while you're driving.

Pursuit of God's plans and purposes
diminishes the hassles, and your hustles.

The past weaves unusual effects into the
fabric of our lives. But, The Master Tailor,
Jesus, creates miracles, signs and wonders
out of every flaw, snag, rip, and tear stain.

Between the promise and its provision
is a problem God will help you solve.

Faith is seeing Light in your heart
though darkness may be all around you.

There are at least two sides to any story.

Never let your enemies appraise you, and
don't take it to heart when they praise you.

Do *your* choices birth profitable returns?
Commit to consult God Who will help to
establish your thinking ~ Proverbs 16:3.

Jealousy keeps you looking at what
you don't have, while blinding you
from seeing what you do possess.

Spiritual maturity is not determined by
the years of one's religious experiences,
but by one's diligent pursuit of God, with
yielded obedience to His Word and His will.

Deception's voice can be subtle, yet
louder than the still, small voice of Truth.

Your independence is solely found
in your total dependence on God.

Weariness leads to weakness in
the body, and distress in the soul.
So WORSHIP, and then, take a nap!

As soon as the re-focus takes place,
the re-vision is inevitable.

Getting better is the result of *receiving*
salvation, correction, deliverance,
healing, truth, and/or change.

To serve God well, know Him well by heart.

PRAY - Until you see every problem is
      always smaller than God!

I AM WELL

Tell me something about yourself
You will be surprised to find
You are much like me.

And I will tell you something of myself
For now I have wealth that I was
Surprised to find for such as me.

You see, I lost my way
But I tell you, I found Him
And now, I am well.

Somehow I know all about you
You've been searching and reaching
For something to hold onto
For something you can have.

But this I know
For I've been out there too
Only to find and learn this teaching
There is nothing to hold onto
There is nothing to have of any worth
Except Him.

You see, I lost my way
But I tell you, I found Him - The Way
And now, I am well.

PROMISES
Or Reasons To Believe
When You Don't Have Any!

"I will be leaning toward you with favor
and regard for you, rendering you fruitful,
multiplying you, and establishing and
fulfilling My covenant with you."
Leviticus 26:9

"There is none like God. . . Who rides through
the heavens in His majestic glory to help you."
Deuteronomy 33:26

"My covenant I will not break, nor alter the
word that has gone out of My lips."
Psalm 89:34

"Fear not, for I AM with you; be not dismayed for
I AM your God. I will strengthen you and harden
you to difficulties, yes, I will help you, I will
hold you up with My victorious right hand."
Isaiah 41:10

"Call on Me, and I will answer you,
and show you great and mighty things,
which you do not know."
Jeremiah 33:3

"For I AM the Lord, I do not change."
Malachi 3:6a

"Peace I leave with you, My peace I give to you; not as the world gives do I give to you. Let not your heart be troubled, neither let it be afraid."
John 14:27

Selah!

COMMIT To BELIEVE, KNOW & TRUST God's Word! God Is Speaking To You Personally. Read, Declare, Then Apply His Text Messages To Your Life, Situations, Challenges, Actions & Aspirations.

TAKE NOTES: HOW Will These Verses Affect Me & My Life?

_____

_____

_____

_____

_____

_____

_____

I Must Challenge
My Obedience To God
To Greater Levels Of Submission. . .

"He must increase, and I must decrease". . . - John 3:30. What I received and *then believed* was an experience of increase in my life. Usually, by faith we believe, then we receive. But God helped me in a very unique way.

When first reading the Verse, I didn't get its full meaning. I pondered, wandering over its compelling directive. It made tracks in my mind and spirit I had to follow. It navigated my course to <u>know</u> God must increase *in me* if my life was ever to become as He promised - given to prosper, to increase in purpose and living life itself! Its truth is we must yield, *out of desire,* to God's preeminence!

If I boast, it's because the revelation of this Verse gifted truth to me! Despite my rereads, I only 'got it' by Grace! God has a way of blessing us though we are blind to our need of His intervening helps. Interestingly, and often, we are absent to acknowledge, by zero gratitude, many of His blessings, mercies and benefits.

The picture was etched. Yield to yield more! Surrender to wield more power! I *wanted* to get what God wanted to give! Indelible impressions were deeply made on my life and in my heart, vastly enlarging my perspectives!

Yielding to this God - Who is above all things, is all power-
ful, knows all things, so loves us, desires to prosper us, IS
The Greatest Giver - can be difficult! You would so think,
'no brainer!' Yet sometimes we reach too low in effort to
grow through and past life's vicissitudes. Our sad excuse:
We *feel* it's easier to trust our own ideas, instincts, sway,
or feelings, than *promises* made by God, Who can supply
credit and character references. Are we so vain to dare
lean on our own insufficient understanding?

Another area of difficulty is our attachment to 'all' we do,
accomplish, or 'where' we are positionally. This causes a
loss of seeing truth - ALL we have *has been given* <u>by God</u>.
Without Him, our significance wanes, even if we're a pope
or a president. To appreciate God, Who He is, and ALL He
does for us, would be a huge reality check. Sorely do we
need a thank-you valve to center us, adjust our sights,
to bring us to our senses and, too, our knees.

Then, of course, we think we have the right of way on the
avenue of control. Our flesh tours us all up in the control
room. We may have the keys or remote, but again, in the
real picture, we have, *by grace,* only what has been given.
It may be difficult to let go of that remote, but it *is* God's
TV, and His show! While it is also difficult to let go of self,
IF we are willing, God IS able to get us up and over ALL re-
sistant, high-up walls! Don't forget, He is <u>for us</u>!

There's much to yield in yielding. One tiny seed or kernel yields lots of seeds and kernels. That death to our flesh, yielding of self, can be done *by faith in God*, <u>with</u> His help. But, giving-up-to-die-in-the-ground will sting, you say? It's a process that, with practice, can be done totally *by means of God's grace* which is totally so sufficient, and doubles as a pain killer. That evil enemy of our soul is the real pain we get to annihilate!

Yielding to God, decreasing, dying to self <u>are</u> producers of a stingless death. "O death ~ O where *is* your sting?" - 1 Corinthians 15:55. Shall we lay it down to allow our God to resurrect a stronger, more effective, Christ centric Believer? It's the yielding that enables the wielding of the fullest power of the Only Living God!

What a great Guy God Is! If we do love Him, are we not to be a bit more willing to obey, follow, listen, and - our fave, surrender *to yield*? YESSS!!! After all, it's His created earth on which we live, His air we get to breathe, and His story we're graced to star in! Reality check!?

Our surrender to God means we get paid now and later! Following God on His paths leads to His heart and to His Presence. The result is *increase* - fruit that remains and recurs, non-stop! Into our hands, hearts and spirits get deposited God's far more profitable returns! AMAZING! O Lord, help us decrease quickly, to increase suddenly!

THE MIND <u>MUST</u> BE RENEWED TO REMEMBER. . .

Matthew 5:14	I am the light of the world.
2 Corinthians 5:17	I am a new creation.
Colossians 2:13	I am alive with Christ.
1 Peter 1:16	I am holy.

THEREFORE. . .

I <u>am</u> a child of God! I <u>am</u> transforming to become my better self ~ who God created me to be!

SUGGESTED CRITICAL READING. . .

The Gospel of John ~ A wonderful New Testament intro. It is considered the Love Book because the most famed, well known Scripture ever quoted is penned within it. . . "For God so loved the world..." - John 3:16. It is here we begin to see the magnificence of Who Jesus Is.

Compared to the other Gospels, John's entry has beauty of its own in that the content's heartbeat is salvation by God's love, and our faith in the Lord Jesus, The Christ!

As you seek spiritual increase, bask in God's presence to enjoy revelations of His heart's passion in every passage. Open your heart to receive the Father's love for you!

Prayer Concerns

_____

_____

_____

_____

_____

_____

_____

_____

_____

_____

_____

_____

_____

_____

Observations & Revelations

_____

_____

_____

_____

_____

_____

_____

_____

_____

_____

_____

_____

_____

Hopes & Intentions

_____

_____

_____

_____

_____

_____

_____

_____

_____

_____

_____

_____

Gratitude Declarations

_____

_____

_____

_____

_____

_____

_____

_____

_____

_____

_____

_____

_____

WHY

Be Hostile,

When You Can Be Happy,

Wholly Healthy, Hopeful, Holy,

And Not Hard To Get Along With!

+

The Vehicle Of Transportation

To This Mind And Attitude Shift Is

PRAYER!

FRIDAYS

Prayer is like a precision tool in the hand of a master craftsman, or a celebrated surgeon, who gently and accurately cuts away the excess particles on a newly excavated rare find, or ravaging cancer cells invading healthy tissue. With the very keen eye of an eagle watching its prey, he, or she, is absolutely attentive to keep the subject intact, whole - sans any breakages, tearing, or unintended severs.

Like separating conjoined twins, the procedure can be long and tedious, and, at times, life threatening. Over and over, again and again, the strokes of this instrument isolate. By cautious care, all intruding, unnecessary elements release at last, freeing to reveal the significantly prized, the purposed, the set apart redeemed, newly made whole, and to God - His precious, His saved, His very own beloved!

With each prayer we remove a layer. With each fervent word we release the captive - freeing the slave of fetters, loosing the ensnared, rescuing the Lord's so greatly loved treasures out of darkness.

Prayer is your gift and position of great power! It is your Divine Connection to The Omnipotent Master over every impossibility, Jesus, Lord God Almighty! O PRAY, Without Ceasing! ~ *1 Thessalonians 5:17*

CONFESSION. . .

I will esteem and value others, as I do myself.

I will pray for others, including my enemies.

I will be a blessing to others, on purpose,
       so that I may glorify God.

RE - SOLUTION

I Resolve: To harbor compassion for everyone ~
           family, friends, associates, and
           people on my life's path.

           To consider the earth, and to never
           take for granted the air I breathe,
           or the environment around me.

HEARS A Word...

It was on the mission field in London, England, when I realized *the responsibility of my salvation*. Not that, prior to this experience, I thought I could chill out and wait up for the rapture. Ever grateful, prayerful, and committed to acknowledge and share God things, were a few ways of efforts I engaged my faith. Adamant to serve and be available, I was an at-your-post God's Girl!

But something unexpected happened. It was a montage of things - signs and wonders, growth and boundary expanding things, yet all sweetly subtle. That Ancient Of Days was leaning in, proving His mercies to be new!

These *things* confirmed the need of the tool prayer is to facilitate the service of ministry's function. It was clear reality, for doing so beckons a greater covering of God's graces! Our prayers were a partnership of agreement to what would be a demonstration of God's intentions.

At each venue, the call was to a much deeper awareness of what was occurring *in the atmosphere*. Like discernment, it was an ushering to a new realm of an unfamiliar greater! It was as if God *had to reveal* His whole heart's outpouring of love for His people amid this new swell of grace. In the awe, we inhaled His fragrant peace bouqueted in boldly expressed compassion.

A great sense of spiritual weight pressed every fiber of my being. I literally, sincerely, wanted to embrace this people, each one! I *needed* to speak out loud of the living love Jesus Is, to pull them from the clutches of a violent enemy, to rush them past fear and the dark! And there, in this Light of God filled room, we stood!

Then, like the dawn of a new day, I suddenly felt the *responsibility of my salvation* stirring new sensitivities in my soul, my heart and mind! The moment was intensely vibrant! I was shaking though standing quite still in the tangible Presence of God, and with tears.

Please hear this truth. Salvation is *given*! It arrives by way of a tremendous, already paid price, with a divine opportunity, no strings, attached. We *get* to be saved, we *get* to serve, as Jesus did so willingly, so excellently. It's the *why* we are Christians! That God would entrust partnership with us - delivering people to Him, helping them to know Him, is a grand privilege of His Grace!

Our *serving* accesses God's power to save and set free others. In short, God saves, blesses and helps us - then we get someone else saved, blessed and helped. HOW can we keep it to ourselves silent, dormant - *without* an attempt to share this incredible miracle? Knowing God is a 'tell-all' journey we are *to gift* others! We must permit His holy fire to be set aflame within us! God's Very Good News Story is the empowerment to declare it!

In your life, or social media sharing moments, who's in the picture? Is it you with a heart to serve God, or your ambition, or to gift God to others? A heart fixed on God is capable of genuine service. For it knows the precious responsibility of real salvation - *the connection of relationship with God*, to be a uniquely personal, vastly important, sought after mantle. God delights in gifting us ALL He is, and ALL He has! Shall we not reciprocate?

You may not be able to evangelize the world but you can be a witness of testimony. You can touch lives with kind, encouraging words, a gesture of compassion, a prayer, a godly life. It makes you a giver ~ just like God! Trust Him to direct you toward a specific help, outreach, or a serving commitment. He is faithful to reward every offering or effort, any gesture and diligence of your heart.

Don't miss the blessing in opportunities to be a blessing! Your deliverance makes you a deliverer. You *overcame* to help others overcome. Your experiences, growth and strengths will reach to teach, and grow to equip so many people - more than you can imagine! Serving makes you a God Distributor when you enable someone's faith walk! It will cause you to reap bountiful harvests when you're planting The Seed - Jesus Christ, in souls!

Share whatever whenever you can. God will return it in pressed down, shaken together, running over measures poured over you, and into ALL your life ~ Luke 6:38!

BEYOND OPINIONS

Each day is the present that comes with
its own presents. Make good use of them all.

You never have to respond to the opposition
with stress, words or worry, just your faith.

God's answer to our prayers may be different
than our original request, but it will always
be better than what we had in mind.

The land of milk and honey has cows and bees!

Take time to hear the music before the song
is over. Take time to listen to the sound
you may have never heard or known.
Hearing is a gift, listening is a skill.

Discipline is an 'I Will' that
constantly supersedes your will.

God's resurrection life causes you
to ALWAYS rise above dead things.

While accomplishing God's purpose,
avoid doing His assignment *your* way.

You are more than your ability, success,
intelligence, history, challenges, or pain.

Obedience to God is a favor magnet.

To love is a command, not a suggestion.

Receiving God's forgiveness, and giving
forgiveness to others and yourself are
foundational acts of faith in Christ.

Potential can be developed by one's
passionate desire to learn and to listen.

With God, it's never too hard, too bad,
too big, too small, or too much. But
don't wait too long getting to Him.

Sweat equity is like the labor that comes
with birthing a baby, or great purpose!

Perfection is never required by God,
only earnest effort and integrity of heart.

Why seek to acquire so much stuff?
Just pursue God! He owns the world,
everything within it, and loves to share!

Remove assumption from your repertoire.

God is the Kaleidoscopic Creator King
of every color, shade and hue.

When you pour out love, you pour in God.

Your decisions should always coincide with
your well thought out plans and preparations.

Avoid attaching emotions to perspectives.

What are you doing with
what God has done for you?

Faux friends are never necessary.

Do the right thing even when
the wrong thing is being done to you.

Correction is enablement, not punishment.
It resets our sights to see what we don't know.

With God's plan of salvation you'll get more
than flares for life's roadside emergencies.
You'll get all the help you will ever need.

The only things we can take with us upon
departure from planet earth are souls
we've won by sharing God's love!

Giving God your reins will help you reign.

No matter how much you know
there's always something new to know.

God says: LOOK UP From Your Phone!

To waiver in faith is to wave favor good-bye.

God doesn't want your 'likes'. He wants YOU!

Pride doesn't mix well with grace.

Some folks know the Word of God,
but His close friends know His voice.

Sometimes we may be overwhelmed.
But at all times, we are to be overcomers.

God won't let you stay blind,
but you do have to open your eyes.

We need spirituality to be fully human
for it is the Spirit of God Who created us.

Nothing about you is insignificant to God.
He made you to be important but not more
important than your purpose, or anyone else.

God's power, peace and provision manifest
when His Word is heard, honored, and obeyed.

PRAY - For clear vision, accurate hearing,
          sound thinking, wise discourse,
          and spiritual understanding.

GOD LITE?

You say your prayers at night
You always bless your food
Sometimes you even lend a hand
You try to fellowship, when you're in the mood
You say, "for Jesus Christ, of course, I stand!"

But when you're left home alone
And you have it all your way
Remember, God is watching you
"Well done, My child!", will He say?

So tell me
Do you want the Light of God
Or do you want God lite
While you're chillin'?

You love to recommend
Your Jesus to your friends
Especially the ones who get your last nerve
You think you're alright
Because most times you're polite
When you have much too much to do to serve.

But what about the time you spend hurting
And searching high and low
For something close to real?

Yet all you find is you
Mourning in the night
And crying to the beat
Of what you cannot feel, nor deal.

So tell me
Do you
Do you want the Light of God
Or do you want God lite?
It's so less filling.

Why don't you taste and see for yourself
That in Him you have been made complete
Make haste and free God from your shelf
You won't even have to be discreet
Why waste another day, my friend
So blessed and beloved are you.

But then
Do you
Do you want the Light of God
Or do you just want God lite?
Are you willing?

PROMISES
Or Reasons To Trust God
When You've Run Out Of Ideas!

"And the Lord said, 'My Presence shall go
with you, and I will give you rest.'"
Exodus 33:14

"No man shall be able to stand before you all
the days of your life. As I was with Moses,
so I will be with you; I will not fail
you or forsake you."
Joshua 1:5

"The God of heaven Himself will prosper us."
Nehemiah 2:20a

"He Who is perfect in knowledge is with you."
Job 36:4b

"He delivered me from my strong enemy and
from those who hated and abhorred me,
for they were too strong for me."
Psalm 18:17

"Show me Your ways, Lord; teach me Your paths."
Psalm 25:4

"If you are willing and obedient, you
shall eat the good of the land."
Isaiah 1:19

"The young lions do lack,
but they that seek the Lord
shall not want any good thing."
Psalm 34:10

Selah!

COMMIT To BELIEVE, KNOW & TRUST God's Word!
God Is Speaking To You Personally. Read, Declare,
Then Apply His Text Messages To Your Life,
Situations, Challenges, Actions & Aspirations.

TAKE NOTES: HOW Will These Verses Affect Me & My Life?

_____

_____

_____

_____

_____

_____

_____

I Must Challenge
My Trust In God
To Greater Levels Of Confidence...

It's true that trust is earned. What does God have to do to earn our trust? What is expected of Him to prove He *IS* qualified to have our complete trust placed in Him?

First of all, He's already done everything. Nothing more is required. Yet He offers His arm of strength to help us, and His enduring love to further draw our trust just to assure us of who we are to Him. What generosity!

While it's difficult for us to grasp our identity, it's also a strenuous stretch to actually trust in God. We bear lots of painful restraint in our lives if we fail to see Who and What we're looking at - God. Even our surroundings tell of what is beyond mere flesh. Uh, maybe God!?

Consistency lends a hand to exacting confidence, so let us ponder a few wonders God *has* performed. Notice a new day and every. (And who else makes days?) So day after day, one after another, they keep coming. The sun has never decided not to rise because of weather, or a 'had-a-late-night-so-I'm-just-too-tired-to-shine' weirdo excuse. Each day shows up, in its own purposed intent, without fail, with no days off, with or without clouds.

And what about the continual obedience of *every* ocean remaining at the shores' boundaries God ordered many millenniums ago? Those waters are wise to obey!

And when taking a new job, we're told of salary, benefits, protocols, etc. We go to work that first day expecting to receive what was agreed, all conditions met, at the time promised. A week or two later, we know there will be an envelope with our name on it. Whether that company is 7-Eleven or the IRS, we know we'll get paid! We totally trust that company's integrity and promise to pay.

WHY is it that hard to trust God? Is that company God? We say we love God, yet we don't fully trust nor believe Him. He loves us despite knowing our doubts, fears, and not-so-nice ways. He gives way more than we thank Him for. He gifts talents and purposes He trusts us with all while we will not trust Him. We're just *not* so sure!?

When the disciples were in the boat, so frightened to see Jesus walking on the water (John 6), He said, "Do not be afraid". That is exactly what He's saying to us *again* - in our now. When whatever we see or know looks scary, He Is STILL God. By His invite, we get seats in heavenly places (Ephesians 2:6), far above the fray, challenges or foes. So please, take note: ALL opposing objects *are always,* for reals, a whole lot smaller than they appear!

We may find it difficult to believe, to get out of the boat, to wait for His comforting answers. But surely, it was also difficult for Jesus to endure the Cross. Yet, He did it, without a murmuring, mumbling, grumbling word. And, ALL while He was dying *for His people* who would doubt Him, or not believe Him at all! With a boldly unflinching spirit of excellence, He surpassed every test in ALL His hard places. He owned His position of utmost difficulty valiantly, and with ceaseless, amazing love.

You CAN choose to get out of the boat of unbelief, fear, indecision, or lack-of-trust, and reach out to Him Who'll never give up on you. He *will not stop loving you*, even while you're *still* sitting in the boat of confusion, uncertainty and contemplation. If you do get scared and nervous, or start to sink as you brave getting out, He won't EVER leave nor forsake you! He won't let go of you, or let you down (Hebrews 13:5b), nor let you drown!

Don't wait another minute, nor waste another day. Why not grow and know God, The Lord, Who desires to show up, show off and show out in all your circumstances, in your whole life, and in all things you, ALL THE TIME!?

You CAN, with the greatest confidence, trust and never doubt Him! Besides, He so loves you and He trusts you! He's your Always Forever Lifesaver Savior! Lift up your voice, Child of The Only Living God, and shout, AMEN!

THE MIND <u>MUST</u> BE RENEWED TO REMEMBER. . .

Psalm 139:14	I am fearfully, wonderfully made.
Jeremiah 1:5	I am approved by God.
John 15:15	I am a friend of God.
Hebrews 2:15	I am set free.
1 Peter 2:24	I am healed.

THEREFORE. . .

I <u>am</u> becoming stronger in wisdom and knowledge
   by the Word of God, and by His grace.

SUGGESTED CRITICAL READING. . .

Choose a Verse to stand on. Can't decide? Ask God!
We need reminders of His promise of faithfulness, especially when faced with problematic people, fearful
times, and other difficulties. By the way, one of His
names *is* Faithful - another reason to praise Him!

You'll be encouraged to hear God's voice in the dark,
or in the midst of madness. It is always calming, liberating and a great assurance. It's like absolute Truth* -
another of God's Wonderful Names you can trust!

* The Truth *that you know* sets you free - John 8:32.

Prayer Concerns

Observations & Revelations

_____

_____

_____

_____

_____

_____

_____

_____

_____

_____

_____

_____

_____

_____

Hopes & Intentions

_____

_____

_____

_____

_____

_____

_____

_____

_____

_____

_____

_____

Gratitude Declarations

_____

_____

_____

_____

_____

_____

_____

_____

_____

_____

_____

_____

_____

STOP Doubting!

START Hoping, Believing & Living

BY *FAITH!*

BEGIN The Journey

BY *PRAYER!*

SATURDAYS

Like Saturdays follow Fridays,
we are to follow after God steadfastly,
consistently, diligently, persistently *always*.

Our decision to do so will determine
where and how far we will go,
and what we will receive
when we get there.

But if we keep getting off the freeway,
and not our purposed exit,
we will arrive late,
or never get to our destiny-tion.

God desires we follow Him
so He can *be with us*
at every point and place in our lives.

It's ALL *ONLY* because
He has an amazingly magnificent plan
to prosper and to bless us
beyond the measure of our greatest hopes
and our wildest dreams!

Jesus Said: "You <u>Must</u> Follow Me."
~ *John 21:22b*

REMEMBER. . .

God's blessings are always at the right time! Timing can mean everything. In due season, the appointed time, the kairos moment... all phrases that emphasize the significance of a God appointment of purpose, importance or destiny. Being prepared is an essential if we are to receive in God's blessing transactions.

Our course of action *must* include engaging the full length of our strengths, doing all we can, yielding to, waiting, and leaning on God in all our ways, *if* we do expect His very best. By our obedience, gratitude, and His graces, we will avail expanded capacities to receive.

These Tools Develop Personal *Stewardship ~ The Required Accountability Of Heart,* For Every Blessing, Benefit And Grace God Very Willingly Grants To Equip, And Empower Us.

RE - SOLUTION

I Resolve: To get out of debt.
　　　　　　To use what I have.
　　　　　　To prepare for increase.
　　　　　　To daily live in gratitude.

HEARS A Word...

Breakthrough is defined as a release, a resolve, a significant change. It can mean overcoming an obstacle or a challenge. It can also be a great miracle, a suddenly!

Do you need one? Are you feeling trapped on all sides by hurts, problems, failure, a hardship or two? Well, it's time to give God your mud pies of complaint and defeat to receive His sweet bread of comfort. IF you allow Him, God will fast forward you beyond the chains, past every bondage, to your release, your breakthrough, your huge breakout! Do you recall He died to set you free?

To forget Whose we are and the credentials of our identity is to allow the enemy to take advantage of our human handicap. If we are hung up in the subjectivity of 'my' issues, 'my' problem, 'my' past, then 'me, my situation and tears', become the focal point, the subject matter. God, our Deliverer is not! Please KNOW, we are the object of ALL His affection, so therefore, we *can* be objective.

We must note, what's happening *in us* is greater than all that's happening to us! It is a 'place' God allows to grant us an *adjusted attention*. He desires to teach us, so we reach our greatest potential of effectiveness in life, in a mess or roles of purpose, and at our post. The 'place' reminds us the war is real, and we need God In every struggle, in the horrors of trauma, and through all our pain.

This perplexing 'place' - the dark tomb of trial, tribulation and trouble is fertile ground, like the womb, out of which God's Resurrection Power re-births our life, and our vision. It's our place of repair while God prepares us for our own, and very personal, breakthrough!

Examine to employ these next strategic components as they are: Decisions For Good Success To Enable Continual, Present Tense, Transforming Breakthroughs.

CONFESSION - of your need for God, with His intervention, in all areas of your life. Take responsibility, ownership - beyond mere regret, for attitudes or actions contrary to His will and plans for your life. Attach genuine repentance, *the* much needed resident of the heart, to gain real, absolute change of mind, behavior, incentive, perspective, and, of urgent need, *to heal.*

COURAGE - to trust, to wait on God to do His part within you *for you.* He only needs your faith. To be humble, in patient, long-suffering and gratitude takes courage <u>if</u> going ahead of God - independent thinking, is the norm. Never forge God's signature on *your* plans, mindsets, behaviors, ideologies, feelings or opinions.

COMPASSION - to pray for others, even enemies, is key to uproot bitterness or animosity, and grow to forgive. Only God Is Perfect! NO judging allowed! Giving mercy is like banking - deposits determine withdrawals. Know <u>always</u> ~ at no time will you ever *not need mercy*!

COMMITMENT - to God, to His ways, His will and Word! Let go of fence-straddling and double-mindedness as a surrender to God. Your consistent, submitted, committed walk of faith, and dying to self DAILY, leads you on paths of new breakthroughs, and transformations into the likeness of Jesus Christ! There, *in Him,* is the peace that surpasses all your understanding, difficulties, trauma triggers, fears, and mindset issues (Philippians 4:7).

These four 'C's' help you foresee possibilities exceeding your own imaginings and knowledge, beyond any obstacles imposing barriers to your faith, or living life as God planned. He will reward you, gifting wisdoms and truth to empower you with *God*-fidence, as He restores your soul - mind, will, and emotions (psyche), resets your vision, and renews to perfect all things you.

Know that foresight is needed to keep your focus, heart, mind and motives forward, and <u>on God</u>. Like the Prodigal came to his senses (Luke 15:17), you will get *to know* your true self, your position of power and identity, with a new freedom. *That* truth leads to experiencing august personal breakthroughs awaiting your faith to find, and your eyes to behold, as you become the recipient of The Lord's promised Abundant Life Plan.

Rally in expectant hope, the breeding ground for countless miracles, and God's 'far more' everything you have never thought of, asked for, imagined, or even dared to dream ~ Ephesians 3:20! He will AMAZE you!

BEYOND OPINIONS

Without prayer, you are a blind soldier, in
an unnecessary war, and without a weapon.

Your faith *in God and yourself* determines
what you'll gain by your obedience and
trust in His Word, plan and purpose.

If you are a teacher, or living on the planet,
always and forever remain teachable.

Knowledge is not the proof of wisdom,
but it is the preparation for prowess.

Avoid the seductions of distractions.

The Word of God is to your spirit
what blood is to your body.

Allow Christ's Mind to precede your mind
for it leads to His inroads of higher thinking.

A challenge is a bridge to a greater success.

Covet humility to stimulate growth, broaden
depth perception, foster integrity, and birth
more capacities for consideration of others.

Goals are NEVER more important than God.

There are NO denominations in Heaven.

If you're running after God - follow close,
stay in your lane, and don't get out of line.

In the face of all its opponents,
real love remains to grow even stronger.

Seven speed bumps on Hell Prevention Road...
The Bible, Holy Spirit, true friends and family,
good conscience, faithfulness, prayers, and
receiving Christ's full Works of The Cross.

To retreat in God equips you
to advance in your life.

God did not bring you this far to leave you
at a bus-stop without a token.

Wait patiently on the Lord, and rejoice while
you wait. He will redeem your wait time
for He Is the Redeemer Who rewards.

Don't worry about tomorrow - Trust God!
He will even help you prepare for it.

Do you give what you want, or what's needed?

A grudge is like grime, or an arrest-worthy crime.

If you've ever been in love, you may have found yourself saying, 'I could just die' to be with that special someone. Know that Someone *did die* just to be with you! It Is A Special Someone Who's Name Is Jesus!

Infusions of God's Word
abate the confusions in your life.

We miss the beauty of the rose if
we only raise complaint for the thorns.

Punishment is penalty for the past,
and correction is training for the future.

Self care helps your spirit, soul and body.

The way you see it may not be the way it is.

Some battles should be fought in silence,
or in the privacy of your prayer closet.

WAIT! Then ask, What Am I Thinking?

At our worst, God still gave His best.

Submission is not subservience.

PRAY - Beyond getting to a blessing,
        but getting to The Blesser.

I BELIEVE

All that I have seen has taught me to believe
in Him Whom I have never seen.

While I've been going places, seeing faces
In all kinds of diverse situations
I've come to know we don't direct this show
I've heard it, I've read it, I've even said it
The Truth Is the Light
This I do so hope you know.

You, whoever you are
Are you the bright, Morning Star?
Can you give tomorrows?
Can you erase sorrows?
And I'm pretty sure you would save me
If you could, if I were drowning
But you don't swim.

Oh, I tell you
All that I have seen has taught me to believe
In Him Whom I have never seen.

The wondrous way that He does it
Like giving us this day
He even gives us what things we need
Oh, I tell you, I declare it, I just love it
Because I can lift my eyes and voice to pray
Oh, how I wish the Pharisees could see.

Indeed, the vast expanses of universes
And the patterns of stars in the sky
Are clear and loudly voluminous clues
That shout a witness of the truth
Besides, there is no profit in a lie
Though well rehearsed
When all the dues have been paid in full
Only by Him, for sooth.

Still somehow silly man thinks he can
Get over on his own
He even boasts to say it
And oh, the attitudes, with no gratitudes
Oh my, oh why are we so rude, so crude
It is a wonder we even get another day.

But the Giver of tomorrow
The One Who can erase sorrow
In spite of us He shows us
His I'm-your-brother way.

All these things are telling me to trust
In Him Whom I have not seen
And in all that I have seen I am taught
For I have learned to believe
In Him Whom I have never seen
I believe, I do so believe
I believe you, too, can believe.

PROMISES
Or Reasons To Believe When It Looks
Like There Are No Reasons To Believe!

"The Lord will fight for you,
and you shall hold your peace
and remain at rest."
Exodus 14:14

"You shall be blessed above all peoples."
Deuteronomy 7:14a

"And all peoples of the earth shall see that
you are called by the name of the Lord,
and they shall be afraid of you."
Deuteronomy 28:10

"Keep the charge of the Lord your God, walk in
His ways, keep His statutes, commandments,
His precepts and testimonies... that you
may do wisely and prosper in all that
you do and wherever you turn."
1 Kings 2:3

"But You, O Lord, are a shield for me,
my glory, and the lifter of my head."
Psalm 3:3

"For the Lord gives wisdom; from His mouth
come knowledge and understanding."
Proverbs 2:6

"For with God nothing is ever impossible
and no word from God shall be without
power or be impossible of fulfillment."
Luke 1:37

Selah!

COMMIT To BELIEVE, KNOW & TRUST God's Word!
God Is Speaking <u>To You Personally</u>. Read, Declare,
Then Apply His Text Messages To Your Life,
Situations, Challenges, Actions & Aspirations.

TAKE NOTES: HOW Will These Verses Affect Me & My Life?

_____

_____

_____

_____

_____

_____

_____

I Must Challenge
My Faith In God
To Greater Levels of Depth & Patience. . .

The Bible says, 'having faith the size of a mustard seed,' is a great power tool (Matthew 17:20). I can really move mountains? That is huge, unfathomable power!

What matters more than having faith is having that faith *in Whom* we believe - God! He's the Whom we ought to believe if we expect to move mountains, or move over.

What's also huge, God gives His power *to us* that He may intervene on our behalf and help us constantly and consistently. Whether we do believe, acknowledge, appreciate it or not, He performs! His incomprehensible power and incomparable love are made manifest to transform us into His likeness, plus, enable us to share, even transfer, these outrageously precious gifts to others!

If we believed God and Who He is, all the world would be changed completely. If we faithed in His faithfulness, all our lives would be limitless. But we waver like fans, from faith to doubt to a maybe, as if God changed like seasons do. We forget, He changes not - Malachi 3:6. He cannot lie - John 14:6. Hebrews 13:8 says: He is forever *always* the same. He owns constancy! We could too *if* we'd just *believe and receive* Him, and all the above, <u>by faith</u>!

131

Why is it *so hard* to believe? We sorta do! Are we afraid, or don't have enough faith to believe everything He said? Is it going to work out for our good no matter what things look like, especially in the heat of our trial? Is He kidding with, 'Fear not!'? Was God pranking us to say He'd never leave nor forsake us? Did God forget how hot the fire of that trial might be? And what if He *'just can't'* like us half as much as we thought? Or maybe, He doesn't give a rip, or a kitty, about the temps in our courtroom?!

The truth of the matter, our faith gets tried in that court-room. Like gold in the refiner's fire, it gets tested, prov-en, as trials go - tried to be true, or not. That heat burns off all traces of our doubts, fears and unbelief. And the greater the heat, the greater the faith emerges. Daddy God is in the waiting room, expectant, longing to see His 'baby', and its beautiful, strong to the core, faith birth.

There, in the place of difficulty, that place of pain, heat and frustration, comes burgeoning forth to fully bloom, what wasn't there before! It's a strength, a trust, a con-viction of confidence, a real, tried and found-to-be-true faith, manifesting in its greatest measure of power!

So when we do login to Supplications@Now.com but no rapid response arrives, no alarms or frets should be our go-to. Nor can we pry replies or blessings out of God's hand. Yes, believing, trusting and waiting are certainly more easily said than done <u>if</u> we are sans patient faith. Isaiah 40:31 says, when we 'wait', God's recompense is a spiritual and physical renewal! Ah, breathe!

In the wait, we can serve up some praises and worship with thanks giving gravy on top! Our 'wait' *blesses* God, *helps* us relax, and *thwarts* the enemy's attempts to defeat us with panic, fear, doubt and discouragement.

God's thoughts and ways are *not* like ours - Isaiah 55:8. Yet His faithfulness <u>is</u> what we're to plant and grow our faith in. And *if* we do, that's when we *will* move so many mountains, do wild exploits like heal and save folk, raise the dead - just to spread His joy! Then, at long last, we will have grown <u>to know</u> this loving, rejection-and-disappointment-free God! It Is He Who *Waits* - with an undisturbed patience, longing for our faith to birth, our eyes to behold Him, as we confess, "Lord, we believe You!"

While we become changed to look like Jesus, walking in our development, growing in strengths and power, our faith *will bloom,* bearing great fruit *as evidence*! Like a fine wine gets better with age, our faith will be stronger, unshakable and unrelenting! That is all because *it was conceived* in the Faithful One, Jesus! It shall yield the *exploits of* nobility! And we shall rejoice in Him, Jesus, The Only Almighty God!!! Sounds like it just might be Tambourine Time, even if ya' got no rhythm!

THE MIND <u>MUST</u> BE RENEWED TO REMEMBER...

Deuteronomy 28:13	I am the head, not the tail.
Galatians 4:7	I am an heir of God.
Ephesians 1:4	I am chosen.
Hebrews 1:3	I am cleansed.

THEREFORE...

I <u>am</u> a believer in God Almighty, Who never changes, Who is making me as He Is in the earth!

SUGGESTED CRITICAL READING...

We need constant reminders to stay our faith in God! It takes courage to refuse engaging with the fake trinity's (world, flesh, and devil) distraction tactics of dismantling our integrity, sound mind, and walk of faith.

To remain stable, we'll need a steady diet of spiritual vitamins and soul supplements found all throughout the pages of God's Word. The Apostles' Letters in the New Testament aid us well along our paths. Paul, especially, has much to say about becoming wealthy in strengths to stand firm with bold, relentless faith.

These tasty morsels will fill you with peace, lead you in the Spirit forward, and shut down all oppositions!

F E E L I N G S

MAY WELL BE FACTUAL.

BUT GOD'S EVERLASTING TRUTH

IS FUNCTIONAL, UNFAILING,

FOUNDATIONAL,

AND FOREVER FRUITFUL!

P R A Y E R

SUMMONS GOD'S SPIRIT OF TRUTH

TO RESTORE YOUR SOUL

AND HELP YOU 'TO FEEL' BETTER!

Prayer Concerns

_____

_____

_____

_____

_____

_____

_____

_____

_____

_____

_____

_____

_____

_____

Observations & Revelations

_____

_____

_____

_____

_____

_____

_____

_____

_____

_____

_____

_____

_____

Hopes & Intentions

_____

_____

_____

_____

_____

_____

_____

_____

_____

_____

_____

_____

Gratitude Declarations

_____

_____

_____

_____

_____

_____

_____

_____

_____

_____

_____

_____

GOD'S PEACE

PREVENTS

PANIC WITHIN.

PRAY FOR IT

DAILY & NIGHTLY!

SUNDAYS

If you rest in God, you will get the rest and best of all He has for you. Rest! And stop running around nonstop in your own strength trying to accomplish everything all the time, every time, resulting in no time to really find out what time it is! Rest to hear, "Be still and know I AM God" - Psalm 46:10.

Even God rested and was refreshed on the seventh day - Exodus 31:16-17. You have a need and a right to rest, chill out, relax, breathe in deep. Everything will be alright *if* you choose to maximize the power of God's ability, and not *only* your own.

God is counting on your *availability* ~ the absolute manifestation of a surrendered will, which can only occur as a result of you not being too 'so busy'. To avail yourself is to access more of His stability!

KNOW ~ It Is God Who began every good working in you. He requires *Himself* to finish the task! Expect Him to do His part. By yielded agreement, you will find yourself less frantic, not frenzied, and a recipient of much more peace. Besides, you are way too blessed to be stressed! Be refreshed, restored and renewed by His sweet, tender love. You are secure, safe in His strong arms, for they are vast with might and strength, and massively immense with power!

REMEMBER. . .

Keep Holy the Lord's Day! God Almighty has
spoken promised blessings for those who do:

"IF you turn away your foot from the Sabbath,
from doing your own pleasure on My holy day,
and call the Sabbath a delight, the holy day of
the Lord honorable and shall honor Him - NOT
doing your own ways, or finding your pleasure,
or speaking your words, *then* you shall delight
yourself in the Lord... I will make you to ride on
the high hills of the earth... I will feed you with
the heritage of Jacob your father. The mouth
of the Lord has spoken." SELAH!
It Is A Prophetic Command. ~ *Isaiah 58:13-14*

RE - SOLUTION. . .

I Resolve: To rest in God, to be still in watchful
silence, and to honor His Presence.

To pray for God's peace to prevail in
my life and environment, my family,
friends, associates and nation, and
all people and places in the world.

To take God's yoke upon me for it is
the weight of His arms around me.

HEARS A Word...

Everything we get from God is predicated on His beyond measure love for us! Why or how He manages to so love us, and so unconditionally, is just so God! The vast multi-facets of His love are unfathomable, and perhaps, some-what confounding to anyone's mind.

One of those facets is His stayed love while we were yet sinners, unlovely and unrepentant. He looked past all of that to give us all this love. At our worst, blind to belief, and boldly wrong, we got His Best - Jesus, and access to the treasuries of all His Graces! How amazing is that?

With all these incredibles, He told us to *be like Him*, and *love like Him*. It's hard enough to love people you must, like the relatives, or nosy, noisy neighbors. He then said, "Love your enemies, pray for whoever persecutes you..." - Matthew 5:44. We *will*, most def, need God for this!

My initial view of this Verse was, for sure, some human error occurred in the original text translations that was not detected over the hundreds of years of reprints. Simply, somebody left out the phrase, 'you don't have to'.

But the truth of it all, the human error was my own. It IS written! Then, I said in prayer, "God, that's easy for You! You are God, thank You, Jesus!" Then, He spoke to my heart, "I *did* say, 'love your enemies.'" Ouch-allujah!

Okay, Lord, but how? "I *can* do all things through Christ Who strengthens me" - Philippians 4:13? Well, okay! It was then I began to understand His 'why'.

God was speaking to my heart that those enemies were actually hurting more than I was (and they should!). I so wanted, "I'll do it later!", to be my hall pass. God's 'want' for me was *to know I needed* to love them, as in hate the sin but love the sinner, as He *always does* with all of us!

The first time I resolved to be big and obey, I will admit, it was hard! It was one of the most difficult efforts of an obedience in all my life. I may have gnashed damage on a tooth trying to utter, "Lord, bless so'n'so... Father, will You help those challenged... Uh, Jesus, have mercy..."!

In the middle of my yielding to obey God, two incredible revelations turned the Light on. And there was a sweet release in my heart that I'd never tasted. I could almost hear wrapping paper tearing away from a present I was about to receive. This God Guy, He IS Greatly Good!

The first revelation brought to mind two Verses, "Be still until I make your enemies your footstool" - Psalm 110:1. And in Romans 12:19, God declares, "Vengeance is Mine, I will repay." Father God always looks out for us. Since God is picky about His kids, He will allow circumstances, issues and people matters to resolve in ways that favor us. It is a grace we do not want to miss!

Add to that Isaiah 61:7's promise of double rewards for our troubles. When God pours out His reimbursements, they show up to be much more than we might hope for.

The second revelation - Jesus loved us, and He died for us when we were *still* God's enemies. He forgave us - in the middle of our mess! Can we forgive? Shall we love the ones exactly as we once were, and often still are?

As I reached to understand God's loving forgiveness, His Spirit captured my soul! This precious gift, now fully un-wrapped, completely opened, so gratefully received, lift-ed weights - hurt, loss, unforgiveness, off my mind, and out of my heart, freeing me to new liberty! Compassion! It elevates the stability and integrity of any relationship, whether family, friends, foes, or God. It heals, like God does, transforming us from deeply within.

If there are difficult people in your life, God will help you love them! (Lunch is optional.) Forgive them! Release it all to God. It will mend your whole heart to see them in a different way, just like God sees you ~ Forgiven!

You may know by now, hurting people hurt people. They need your help, and your God. Allow His love *within you* to be a real blessing of healing and transformation, and a recompense *to you* - the forgiven. In this process, you'll look exactly like Jesus because you have REIMBURSED GOD, BY BECOMING A FORGIVER ~ Just Like He IS!

HEARS Another Word...

Are you waiting for an answer to a prayer? What if The Promises of God got released suddenly to flow over all your life? Would you like such a miracle to land right in your face? Well then, you've got to *WORSHIP God*!

Somehow we omit this significant, privileged *mandate* on our gotta-do list. We read and/or study God's Word (sorta), do church, pray/prey, but we don't *do* HIM as we ought, nor without an 'I want' attached.

Thinking of how needy we are to be acknowledged and appreciated, shall we profess God's works that clearly prove Him so very worthy of all our homage, gratitude and total praise? Surely, worship *is due* Him!

God inhabits the praises of His people (Psalm 22:3)! He *manifests <u>in</u> our worship* - our personal praise, which is a prerequisite to inviting entry of God's Presence. The result is God's Anointing - His G*iftings,* released onto us, in our lives and circumstances, repositioning us into His higher spiritual realms. Simply, God pours His Superior Spirit onto our lesser natural, creating His supernatural 'special effects' *only* He can expend and release over us. It is our worship that ushers us into this *holy place*!

True worship draws the heart of God to beget relation-ship beyond any religious experience. Its intimacy fuels a heart's fire to incite an intentional focus *on God*! As our eyes are upon Jesus, the whys and sighs of our flesh, and lies of the enemy are nullified. Those noises cannot remain the main distraction. Each time we say His Name, Jesus, He gives His undivided, omniscient, and personal attention! But does God have our undivided, committed to know Him, fully present and personal attention?

It's very clear. In order to relate, there must be time set and spent with the subject being related to, or relation-ship is not established. How much time do we give God? Remember, He gave us ALL the time we have! Perhaps we might, at least, maybe, tithe our time!?

And we're so selfie! We can't find any focus on His love amidst our murmurs, whines, complaints, and stuff. But if we'd <u>think</u> *about His love*, it just might stir our passion. What if we worshiped God with all our heart? That could remind us of His benefits, and many countless kindness-es, graces and mercies. That would bring us to a deeper longing for Who God Is, and eliciting our heart's yield in a prostrated pursuit of His very presence!

We are made to give God our love, affection, and all our sincere worship. Generous in love, God longs *for us!* HIs desire *is us*! He made us to give Him our love in return - as our own preferred, very personal mandate.

I once read that worship ascends like arrows piercing the heaven's clouds, allowing God's abundance to rain down.

Certainly then, worship profits us! So we *owe* God for ALL He is, for ALL He constantly gives and does for us.

Another grace, our worship posture is a war strategy to draw God nigh and shield us in the trenches. No enemy can invade God's Presence. It might sound crazy to be so praise-y when in challenge, or a battle. But God lifts us up and out of those 'pit'-iful traps while our 'worship ascends like arrows', pouring from our lips sacrificially, up and out from the depths of our hearts!

The heart is the most important instrument of worship. Until our hearts fall at His feet, we will cry still, "I have fallen, and I… !" Who hasn't been in a trauma's drama? A broken heart is a language God deeply understands, and always, always longs and desires to mend.

As we draw closer, worship changes us under the *great* of God's glory. We're made more complete, honorable, profitable, holy and useful to Him. Our worship renders us pristine, well enabled in all our life's postures.

Will you worship God Who gives life abundant, limitless, unending and eternal? Can you hold Who proffers total answers to resolve all your scary dilemmas? Why can't you pause from your weary world to engage God's King-dom Wonders? WORSHIP Him Who made you To BE <u>His Own Child</u> ~ A Joint Heir *With* Jesus, The Christ, Who IS The Only Begotten Son Of The Father ~ Romans 8:17!

BEYOND OPINIONS

Your life's assignment is to FAIL NOT.

Never resist or resent the trying of your faith.

God plans new things, beyond our knowledge, intellect and learned experiences, so we will partner with Him and, by Him, accomplish.

Sometimes less is more ~ the less you sin, the more pleasing to God you are. The less you fill yourself with you, or the things of this world, the more God will delight in you and graciously supply all your need.

Raise your expectations, confidence and faith to the level of never giving up on what God promised, for you know He will perform.

Every challenge, difficulty or problem has an attached lesson, truth and blessing.

Obedience is an acquired skill, and a required decision.

Under the circumstances is a must climb over.

FOCUS to see a future greater than your history.

The greatest promises often manifest *after*
the most cringingly crazy and chaotic delays.
Wait for it, while you give God praise on credit!

The move forward can be a difficult challenge.
But God gives stability to grow up, leap forth,
never quit, and resist ever falling backwards.

Misunderstanding to far too many is actually,
and unfortunately, their own understanding.

The Word has deep pockets of wisdom, truth,
help, hope and refreshing. Read, and re-read it!

God rewards the pursuit of Him (Hebrews 11:6)!

Worship lifts us up, over and beyond every
battle, limitation, difficulty, struggle, or assault.

Transition is not the same as change.
It's the grace by which we acclimate to change.

Never do the right thing at the wrong time, for
the wrong reason, or with the wrong person.

Efforts without results are invalid practices,
making invalids of us if we continue.

Blessings can often be encased in trouble,
like raw honey is surrounded by bees.

FYI - Partial obedience is disobedience,
and delayed obedience is dishonor.

Prayer is your Declaration of Dependence.

God is not required to act in the possibles
for He alone Is God of the impossibles.

Favor is never a coincidence.
It is God's will, way, grace and kindness.

Avoid being planted in the inadequate soil
of fruitless, non-reciprocal relationships.

To know God is to NEVER stay the same.

Whatever didn't work in *your* plan was either
too small, or didn't match God's plan for you.

Our blessings may be specific to our need,
but they are not exclusive to us. We are
blessed to become greater blessings.

Redirect the intentions of your actions
from performance and transactions
to acts of service and generosity.

Doubt, worry and fear pollute faith and life.

To grow in relationship with God, study to
know the Bible, for it Is God Himself IN PRINT!

No matter how you feel, what is said or done
against you, or the obstacles to overcome,
your purpose remains and will manifest.

Ignorance can be as dangerous as willful evil.

Aim to be righteous rather than to be right.

Read God's Word to be equipped with
the wisdom and insight to read the
rooms you are called to enter.

Sometimes being on the ground
is the only place we will absolutely
appreciate the grace of standing up.

God is complex, but never complicated
confusing, inconsistent, limited, or wrong.

Pride is a preventer of spiritual growth
because it is an advocate of self-sufficiency.

Have faith in God! Who else Is Omnipotent,
Omniscient, Omnipresent, creates universes,
and owns all things above, in and on the earth?

Some are committed, and less are submitted.

As you Pray, BREATHE! Relax to rest in God's
Presence with love, trust, worship and awe.

THE MAN FROM NAZARETH

I know Somebody Who
Can take good care of you
No matter what state of mind you're in.

Life Assurance is His plan
The premium is paid as only He can
He guarantees to see you through
The danger, the trouble, the thick or thin.

He is the Man from Nazareth
The One Who raised Lazarus
Grace is His game
Forever He Is the same
Jesus, the Wonderful, is His Name.

When I was about to break
And life was too hard to take
With no place to go
As a friendless nobody
His words captured me
He said, "I lived to die to make you free
And give you life abundantly with no end."
He rescued me
From the hell of a lonely sadness
He redeemed my life, my soul, my mind
From the darkness of madness.

I was cast down to the ground
Lower than the bass part
When I lifted my eyes and found
The only Knower of the heart
The Mender of the torn apart.

He's the Man from Nazareth
The One Who raised Lazarus
Grace is His game
His friendship I claim
Always and forever He is the same.

He will take good care of you
For He is Somebody Who
Loves unconditionally and for true
His power to help you will forever endure
For it is unfailing and your only real cure.

He is the Man from Nazareth
The One Who raised up Lazarus
His grace you can claim
Because yesterday and today
Tomorrow and forever
He is still now and always the same
Jesus, the Wonderful, the Forever Lover
The Keeper of your heart, mind and soul
Jesus, Precious Jesus Is His Great Name.

PROMISES

Or Reasons To Believe The Only One
Who Never Lied, And Never Will.

"I will both lay down in peace, and sleep, for
You alone, O Lord, make me dwell in safety."
Psalm 4:8

"Weeping may endure for a night,
but joy comes in the morning."
Psalm 30:5b

"The steps of a good man are ordered by
the Lord, and He delights in his way."
Psalm 37:23

"By the help of God I will praise His word; on
God I lean, rely and confidently put my trust;
I will not fear. What can flesh do to me?"
Psalm 56:4

"Because you have made the Lord your
refuge, even the Most High, your dwelling
place, no evil shall befall you, nor shall
any plague come near your dwelling."
Psalm 91:9-10

"He has removed our sins as far away
from us as the east is from the west."
Psalm 103:12

"This is what the Lord says
Who made you and formed you in the
womb, Who will help you: 'Fear not.'"
Isaiah 44:2a

"Instead of your shame you shall have a double
recompense; instead of dishonor you shall rejoice
in your portion. Therefore in their land they shall
possess double; everlasting joy shall be theirs."
Isaiah 61:7

"Behold, I AM the Lord, the God of all flesh.
Is there anything too hard for Me?"
Jeremiah 32:27

"For He Himself has said, 'I will not in any way
fail you nor give you up nor leave you without
support, I will not in any way leave you helpless
or forsake you nor let you down.' So we boldly
say - 'The Lord is my Helper, I will not be afraid.
What can man do to me?'"
Hebrews 13:5b-6

"For the Lord Himself will descend from heaven
with a shout, with the voice of an archangel
and with the trumpet of God. And the dead in
Christ will rise first. Then we who are alive and
remain shall be caught up together with them
in the clouds to meet the Lord in the air.
And thus we shall always be with the Lord."
1 Thessalonians 4:16-17

"No eye has seen, nor ear heard, nor
the heart of man imagined, what God
has prepared for those who love Him."
1 Corinthians 2:9

Selah!

COMMIT To BELIEVE, KNOW & TRUST God's Word!
God Is Speaking To You Personally. Read, Declare,
Then Apply His Text Messages To Your Life,
Situations, Challenges, Actions & Aspirations.

TAKE NOTES: HOW Will These Verses Affect Me & My Life?

_____

_____

_____

_____

_____

_____

_____

The "I's" Of God

"I AM with you and
I will watch over you wherever you go."
Genesis 28:15

"I will set him in the safety for which he yearns."
Psalm 12:5b

"I will instruct you and I will teach you in
the way you should go; I will counsel you
and I will guide you with My eye."
Psalm 32:8

"I, even I, AM He Who blots out your
transgressions... I will not remember your sins."
Isaiah 43:25

"I will carry you and I will rescue you."
Isaiah 46:4b

"I have engraved you on the palms of My hands."
Isaiah 49:16a

"I AM ready to perform My word."
Jeremiah 1:12b

"I AM with you ALWAYS."
Matthew 28:20b

I Must Challenge
My Integrity In God
To Greater Levels of Excellence. . .

We are to "walk as children of Light" - Ephesians 5:8, *IF* we are real Christians. Sometimes that gait is more like a limp, or waddle, because we're not standing erect and sure in our posture of belief. We might be adulting - in our age bracket, but we have not made the grown-ups list in our faith's tracking to BE believable believers.

If our talk doesn't match our walk, we'll sound *kinda* like church but look suspect, and far from it. Our lips praise God, while our actions raise eyebrows. Sunday's hymns become weekday hmmms! What are we thinking? What are we up or going down to? Do we identify with God, or are we showing up with our 'I-got-this!' mentality?

What happened to effecting folks so they see Jesus? It's a 'call' that provides God's love and efficacious Blood to cover us if, or when, we do get spinach in our teeth, or a faux pas attempts to shade our swag. Our purified heart gets to shine through despite the frailty of our flesh.

When our heart's condition is uncompromising, we show off the finer stuff. Like a tea bag in hot water yielding its inner essence, and all it's made of and for, our heart renders its content - ALL it's made of and for: GOD!

The clear and simple truth of the matter, our heart was made to be full of God, His love and postures. When it is, it shows a better design, like signage. Never will it be distorted, discolored or influenced by the flesh or its inconsistencies. Constanly, it bouquets its very Precious Content - God *Himself*. It's fragrantly sweet, just as is the knowledge of God (2 Corinthians 2:14)!

If our spiritual integrity adheres to Kingdom mores, we will arrive to exhibit God in our person. Then, what we stand for can stand up against all compromise, and any temptation to 'Baal' from God's image on and within us.

Within the parameters of a believer's integrity lies a virtue of a righteousness outweighing being right. It's ever seeking the better thing. This pursuit is impassioned as the heart becomes fully ceded to its Resident, the Holy Spirit, for and by Whom it was created.

On our own, we are left with, or coerced by, destructive disinformation and misunderstanding. But if we look up to God and His hills from which comes ALL our help, His Spirit pours on what is itself deficiency. There He *forms excellence within us,* our spirit, and on our whole life.

Our absolute acceptance of God develops *to refine us,* transforming us to a higher standard of an integrity created and imparted to us *By God Himself!* Live To STAY In God's Divine Light, And His All-Empowering Benefits.

THE MIND <u>MUST</u> BE RENEWED TO REMEMBER. . .

Romans 8:28	I am called, set apart.
Galatians 3:9	I am blessed.
Philippians 1:6	I am confident.
2 Timothy 1:7	I am not afraid.
Revelation 21:7	I am victorious.

THEREFORE. . .

I <u>am</u> constantly and forever so loved by God,
tho in my weaknesses, I <u>am</u> undeserving.

SUGGESTED CRITICAL READING. . .

God is very clever. Whenever you want a fresh word, He more than obliges. If you are stuck in a quagmire of unresolved issues or questions, you only need to ask because God IS The Answer, and The Help!

Open the Word for a response, encouragement, a cool drink in your drought, fresh bread in a famine, rest in a weary wilderness. God's Word is alive, refreshing, and forever Truth. It provides a way - with power, wisdom, and insight, out of every no-way, no-win situation.

God's Holy Spirit will guide you into all understanding. Ask - you will receive. Always precede your asks with your praise because God is waiting to bless you!

Prayer Concerns

Observations & Revelations

_____

_____

_____

_____

_____

_____

_____

_____

_____

_____

_____

_____

_____

Hopes & Intentions

_____

_____

_____

_____

_____

_____

_____

_____

_____

_____

_____

_____

_____

Gratitude Declarations

_____

_____

_____

_____

_____

_____

_____

_____

_____

_____

_____

_____

"TAKE REST...

A Field That Has Rested

Gives A Bountiful Crop."

O V I D

DAILIES

REMEMBER: Acknowledge God in all your ways, in all you do, and in all things concerning you.

Lean *not only* on your understanding, opinions, thoughts, knowledge, assumptions or abilities.

Always engage in truth ~ for truth tends justice, and draws an accountability to sound thinking.

Pray without ceasing ~ but pause to hear God's still, small voice. As you do, bear compassion for others, family, friends, foes, and those in need of the knowledge and mercies of God.

Be a worshiper in all things you as a lifestyle. Worship is a shield against anxiety, doubt, fear, arrogance, jealousy, and confusion.

Be responsible to care for yourself and prosper in health - the wealth of body, soul and spirit.

Be teachable and more than willing to change. Be skilled to hear more than your own voice. These Keys avail you to wisdoms that lend ability to become mindful in heart, mind, decision making, and regard for others.

Lighten Up! NO dimmer switches allowed.

REMEMBER: Own humility, and avoid boasting!
Then you will be heard when you are seen.

KNOW: God looked past your faults to serve your
need, and form you as righteous. Look past you
or your circumstances *to see God* Who is well
able to sustain you, your life, and to help in
or through any difficulty or challenge you
may face! PRAISE GOD AT ALL TIMES!

Be intentional to develop your integrity and
character for they confirm your greatness!

When *you have a need*, plant seeds of time, joy,
efforts, earnest consideration, prayer, peace,
hope, money, and give more than you take.

Praise God in all things, for it is a principle
designed to prosper those who comply.

When you speak and declare God's Word DAILY,
it will build and sustain you, your faith and life.

Allow God's Will to preempt your plans,
mindsets, methods and preferences.

Impulse is not the same as intuition, or instinct.
Seek God's Counsel *before* making major change.

Don't just use your head. Apply your heart!

REMEMBER: The most fragrant and precious
flower in the garden of life is gratitude.

Being out of order will lead you out of favor.

Hold your head up - it is the direction
to which you should forever be en route!

Thank God always because giving thanks is
an investment that returns supernatural
measures of increase, favor and power.

Allow God's Holy Spirit to be your Guide
through all the journeys and safaris of life.

See your purpose as greater than your pain,
sin, mistakes, challenges, inabilities or prowess.

While in the storm, take courage and choose
to pursue, promote and remain in peace.

Obedience is NEVER an optional Plan B.

Trust God to be your Holding Space ~
A Place of safety and peace where
you will never fail or fall apart.

Love yourself in all the turns of transition.

Love God for Who He Is *above* all He does.

SELAH *

Be Aware And Willing To Know

The Power Of FAITH In Almighty God!

Be Deliberate To Develop Your Faith

Personally, Mindfully, And Sincerely

With Passion, Yet Without Doubts Or Fears.

PRAYER ~ Conversations With God,

Enable Faith To Grow

With Contagious, Ardent Love And Zeal.

* Pause & Calmly Think On These Things.

DAILY & NIGHTLY. . .

<u>DECIDE</u> to humble yourself, to bless and encourage your whole life by choosing to ALWAYS Remember and Know, with all your heart, soul, spirit, and by your lifestyle, this Truth: It Is God's Mercy of Patience poured on you *while* He waits for you to know Him, without any doubt, and to BELIEVE HIM! You and Your Faith Are His Utmost Desire! And never forget that Jesus DIED TO BE WITH YOU!

<u>REALIZE</u>, God Waits For You ~ **every minute** of each day and night, in the times absentmindedness intrudes or in the *whens* you fail to follow the paths of His leading. All while He ceaselessly remains with you, He *chooses* to re-mand you to the custody of His full, attentive protection and care. He provides ALL He gives <u>because</u> of His ever-lasting, unfailing, unconditional love *for YOU*!

<u>YOUR TASK IS:</u> To Know, Believe, Love, Trust and Follow God with the urgent necessity of every breath you take.

God calls you by name to BE the greatest expression of who you are. Answering His summons to this eminence means abandoning the lessers ~ what <u>you</u> cannot do, or have been denied access to, what you think impossible, and every other trauma, plot, or destructive intentions aimed to annihilate your life's future. It Is fully Possible *IF* You Simply REMEMBER: GOD CALLS YOU <u>HIS CHILD</u>! BE INTENTIONAL & GRATEFUL TO ANSWER THAT CALL!

In the greater iterations of your full identity, truth, value and worth, you *shall discover* there IS The Great WITHIN you - *what God had in mind from the beginning of time:* the Reflection and Image of Himself, uniquely, masterfully designed and divinely expressed within YOU, His Child. You *shall see* <u>to know</u> it for yourself, with your own eyes!

In the good days, through the weighty challenges, or uncertainties of life's seasons, I pray you will find God in all the mixtures of all your life's moments.

My hope is you'll never let go of God's incredibles within you. Allow your heart to overflow with truth, peace and hope authored by God Himself, expressed in great, ever growing, and vastly abundant measures!

May you be a vessel through which God shines His Light to distribute and demonstrate His Power. BE A Diffuser of His heavenly fragrance, never a confuser. Let the real Gospel of salvation, love, truth, deliverance, healing and power be your passion to share with the masses, and all those you have been called to bless with our Great God!

In conclusion, and with an Amen. . .
Please accept the content within these pages as spiritual food without the bones of any religious overtones.

God bless you day after day after day after day after day!

FOR GOD SO LOVED YOU...

THAT HE GAVE

HIS ONLY BEGOTTEN,

HIS SON JESUS, THE CHRIST ~

SO THAT IF YOU WOULD

ONLY BELIEVE HIM,

YOU WILL NEVER, EVER PERISH,

BUT YOU WILL HAVE

ETERNAL, EVERLASTING LIFE.

JOHN 3:16

Special Thanks & Appreciation...

In this book, Pastor Ivory keeps us focused on the One True God, the Source of all we are, what we have, and all wisdom. We get to *know* that God loves us. So if we put God first, all else will follow.

It was good for me to read it!

Norma J. Williams
Attorney At Law

Pastor Ivory has taken me on a magical journey of God's love for us. This book, which is filled with many anointed words, has inspired me, encouraged me, humbled me, and given me more peace.

Whether you're already walking with Jesus, or would like to begin a journey with Him, this is your book! One of my favorite passages: *Retreat in God to advance in your life.*

I am more empowered now to share the Word of God.

Linda Colucci-Madalone
Author

To God be the glory! It is quite a privilege to experience such wonderful messages and Scriptures that, even as I now speak, continue to bless my heart.

"VIEWS" will guide each and every reader through their personal spiritual growth. Thank you for taking time to help us through our daily faith journey!

Dr. Rhoda Ann-Michaux James
Doctor of Educational Leadership
University of LaVerne

More About The Author...

IVORY STONE is a decades long Entertainment Industry veteran! Her credentials include stage, TV, studio performances with such iconic artists as Motown's Diana Ross, Smokey Robinson, Stevie Wonder, and other legendaries.

Broadening her reach, Ivory is now the published author of her fourth book, with more upcoming.

Founder of Cornerstone Worx, a re-education counseling outreach, Ivory uses her wealth of tools and experiences to assist others beyond survival to real recovery. An advocate for personal discovery of self-worth, dignity and identity, Ivory is well aware of these invaluable tools, for they are necessities to living a full and restored life.

Imparting the relevance of esteem, compassion and consideration for all peoples into her work, ministry, serving, artistry, and endeavors is a mandated core value for this dynamic creative. A Pastor, Writer, Author, Bible Ethics Teacher, and Speaker... just to name a few, are postures of position that are her passion and pursuits!

Ivory Stone lends a dynamic extension of faith to readers throughout the pages of VIEWS. She encourages a committed, deeper *know* of God and His love to forge an empowering and personal grasp of VIEWS' greater answers, insights and hope!

AT THE DOOR

Visions In Excellence Journals

www.ingramcontent.com/pod-product-compliance
Lightning Source LLC
Chambersburg PA
CBHW030257130626
46549CB00002B/568